ENJOY YOUR
HOUSE PLANTS

A window garden framed with vines and glowing with flowers is always a focus of interest. Hobby collections of lustre or glass combine delightfully with the plants.

ENJOY YOUR HOUSE PLANTS

By
Dorothy H. Jenkins
and
Helen Van Pelt Wilson

Photographs by Gottscho-Schleisner

Drawings by Joseph Schultz

NEW YORK

M. BARROWS & CO., INC.

First Printing, July 1944
Second Printing, December 1944
Third Printing, February 1945
Fourth Printing, August 1945
Fifth Printing, July 1946
Sixth Printing, December 1947
Seventh Printing, April 1949
Eighth Printing, November 1950

PRINTED IN THE UNITED STATES OF AMERICA
BY AMERICAN BOOK—STRATFORD PRESS, INC., NEW YORK

CONTENTS

5

ENJOY YOUR
HOUSE PLANTS

CHAPTER I

THE PLEASANT POSSIBILITIES
OF PLANTS INDOORS

"THERE is no such thing as a house plant," said an enthusiastic outdoor gardener some years ago. In the literal sense that no plant can claim a house for its native habitat, as ferns belong to the woods and cacti plants to the desert, he is correct. But some ferns come out of the woods to thrive indoors and certain cacti tolerate four walls and a roof. In fact, the list of plants which will grow in the house given half a chance is a long one. The list of people who have grown them well is even longer.

Today the decorative possibilities of house plants are only just being realized. A few geraniums or vines scattered about rooms can be interesting to those who are growing them. But the odd plant here and there does not add up to an artistic experience.

Take, however, a bright and pleasant window, design it for the display and contentment of plants, arrange therein a seasonal series of color schemes to match or complement the colors of a room, apply the rules of emphasis and succession so effective in the garden out of doors and then something definitely ornamental will emerge. Such a winter garden is not only a constant pleasure to look at but it is fun to care for too. You will be surprised at how much a window garden contributes to the homelike atmosphere of a house.

One of our gardens, for example, is made up of two large window arrangements separated by a door. Whether there's a white blizzard whirling outside, gray sheets of rain or blue sky and clouds, we see the landscape through a green leafy vista. And, since one of these windows is on the axis of the hall, no visitor ever crosses the front door threshold without having a pleasant and refreshing glimpse beyond of riotous vines, feathery ferns and red, yellow, pink or lavender blooms according to the season. And they all enjoy it — the postman with letters, the milkman collecting his bill, and all our friends who lingeringly sip a glass of sherry or a cup of tea at the table beside our gay winter windows.

Such gardens as ours are, of course, possible for anyone who has a *light* window. It need not even be sunny and may be quite cold or quite warm. It's all a matter of recognizing and evaluating such factors and then either removing or outsmarting the difficult ones. Thus we take down our glass curtains; that's removing in quest of more light; and we put pebble trays over radiators; that's outsmarting in the interests of humidity.

Even in a city apartment a window garden is possible. With no outdoor site for reconditioning plants in summer, no cool cellar for resting them, however, the mortality rate will be higher. When conditions are thus limited, plants must be carefully chosen according to the light possibilities of the available window and also for their general durability, if the temperature of the apartment is likely to soar. With a frame of such enduring vines as grape ivy or philodendron and with the smaller foliage plants as background, a city window may prove a most satisfactory home for house plants. Here wax begonias or yellow marguerites are introduced for color and an occasional gay flowering plant from the florist for delight, however brief.

So if you like to amuse yourself with plants indoors, highlighting the Christmas season with poinsettias, or cheering yourself up through drab February with primroses and cyclamens, look over the possibilities of your apartment or house and select a window for your venture.

If a window garden is neither desirable nor possible, many places in a room cry out for even a single plant. A coffee table, a mantelpiece or bookcase, perhaps the desk may all be appropriately graced. It's quite possible to keep a plant happy though isolated.

Growing things indoors is a delightful hobby to combine with china or glass collecting. The decorative window may be designed to include a limited number of plants with some sparkling blue Stiegel or crystal clear Waterford on the upper shelves. Perhaps a row of quaint luster pitchers is to be lined up above a display of ferns or a china Virgin with attending angels and candles placed with the poinsettias for the holiday season.

With a woman's passion for change we frequently alter the special aspects of our decorative windows. A Copenhagen head of a small boy, a blue veiled madonna or a golden "Unknown Lady" flanked by tall brass or squat pewter candlesticks, a copper coffee pot, gleaming red goblets, an antique black sugar bowl and a pair of turquoise satin-glass bowls are other treasured items which at different times we have enjoyed combining with plants. When such interesting reminders of our travels or our families are included, we find it effective to place among them a few specimen plants of vivid silhouette value. An aloe or a columnar *Euphorbia lactea* have strong interesting forms to view against the light.

Although we have also included animal forms of fine china — we do have a kitten collection which we incline to scatter among our plants about Valentine's Day and there's a nice assembly of carved wooden horses appropriate somehow to October — we avoid too many kinds of unrelated objects displayed at the same time. At this point we wish to go on strong-minded record that we consider tortured shapes of camel or faun bearing suffering succulents and vines indiscriminately about their persons, as not at all our idea of proper companions for our elegant and dignified ferns, ivies and begonias. And we also consider it an insult to a fine plant to wrap the base in stretched crêpe paper or basket-weave covers of strident hue.

In other words, we strive in our indoor gardens for the quality of distinction. Only fine ornaments are admitted. Only the most healthy and handsome plants remain. They must be in proportion to the measurements of a garden, too. Once they've become fair, fat and forty, requiring large containers and greater growing space, we school ourselves to hardheartedness. We make a few cuttings and then give the plant to the nearest hospital or unsuspecting friend.

Our ideal garden in the house is therefore by no means a collection of oddments. We try to achieve a calculated and unified design, with each beautiful plant and every item of china or glass an important contributing element to a satisfying whole.

CHAPTER II

THE WINDOW GARDEN
BECOMES A REALITY

A COLLECTION of plants growing in pots and scattered helter-skelter all over the house, or a window garden? The decision is yours. For our money, the window garden, as you may have guessed, is fascinating both in its reality and its construction.

A plain window which is about to perform a Cinderella act must first be equipped to hold plants. The sill is a logical place to start. When it is deep, as in stone houses, a ready-made space is at hand. In this case nothing more than selecting the right plant for the exposure and fixing the pebble-filled saucer that belongs underneath it is absolutely necessary.

Most houses, however, have the more orthodox narrow window sill, about three inches wide. This sill will hold small plants (and two- or three-inch pots with their saucers) but there is no room to play around with arrangements. The simplest answer to a narrow sill is a braced board shelf fastened on a level with the sill as an extension. If men in the family don't take kindly to a little carpentry, extension sills may be purchased. One that adds on four inches is adjustable from twenty-four to forty-eight inches in length.

A one-level picture, depending on the window sill only, is inadequate and, furthermore, permits the enjoyment of only a few plants. A satisfactory window garden must be a complete picture. At this point our hunt revolves around shelves that can be placed in the upper part of the window. It doesn't matter whether your window is outsize, average or dwarf, casement or regular sash. Firms specializing in shelves will build them to fit your odd-sized windows and ready-made, hanging shelves are available for casements. For everyday windows, the gamut runs from the simple glass medicine shelf to trick ones adjustable in length and fitting around curtains.

Narrow, short glass shelves from the neighborhood drugstore or hardware shop are most effective. Simple brackets will hold them at the latch strip line and in between, both above and below this median, as in our larger window garden. The shelf story doesn't end, however, in the corner drugstore. Hanging shelves, which can be suspended from the cross bar, are beautifully made with wrought iron, carved wood or plain metal supports that give a clean, modern feeling. Collectors of colored glass, animals or miniatures use this type shelf, too, but they are equally appropriate for small plants such as cacti and strawberry begonias. More substantial full-width shelves come ready-made in several variations adjustable in length and attached in different ways.

When the right shelves have been placed, the window frame is considered. It is a simple matter to string double lengths of strong cord or picture wire which is attached to two- or three-inch staples along three sides of the window frame. These guide the long reaches of ivy or philodendron and so frame our living picture with alluring green.

Brackets add grace and an accent point of another sort. They are even more attractive and diversified than shelves. Placed in asymmetrical balance along the window frame, they will hold pots of "the gadding vine." Our chief pride and joy are the old kerosene lamp holders which we discovered in a corner of the cellar several years ago. Painted soft green and attached to the front of the window frame, they are perfect supports for a pot of plumbago in flower or one of the star begonias.

Plant stands and metal flower boxes fill in that empty space between window and floor if a radiator doesn't complicate matters. A box can be a delightful mass of greenery and flowers. Stands, varied in their design to suit all sorts of décor from Adam to Modern, hold one to eight flower pots. They add an especially gracious note to bay windows.

If the window garden is above a radiator (not the best spot although we have had window gardens that fought and won this battle), insulating material such as a thick layer of rock wool is fitted over the radiator. Then this becomes the ideal place for a plant tray. If

either zinc or galvanized iron is available, the plumber
or roofer makes an inch-deep tray to fit over the radiator
cover and the insulating material. This tray, after a wash
of hydrochloric acid (just dip a cloth in a solution
made up of one teaspoon to one cup of water) is also
given a coat of aluminum radiator paint so that the
finishing coat, which matches the woodwork, will stick.
When it has been put in place, the tray is filled with
white roofing pebbles or those small stones in which
narcissus bulbs are planted.

On this layer of stones the plants are set. As they
are watered, excess moisture runs down into the pebbles and additional water is poured over them daily as a
source of constant humidity for the plants. Often the
house plant addict who previously has admitted "no luck"
discovers that it wasn't luck but humidity that was lacking. A constant source of evaporation was the something
more that needed to be added.

This tray idea brings us right back to the window sill
where we started. A tray is one of those necessities if
the window garden is located over a radiator; it is a
nicety for a sill of any sort with or without bottom
heat. It makes plants a tidy matter with no splashing
on woodwork or floor when the rounds are made with
a watering can and it provides a nice solid foundation
on which to start arranging an indoor plant picture.

Trays, shelves, plant stands, brackets and — by no
means least — the wire or the cord that holds the vine
frame together, all these are the structural details which
make it simple to find a six- to nine-months home for

that collection of plants one gathers in the fall. Such is the practical basis for enjoying your house plants when on a winter day tender green tendrils are put out by flourishing vines, the geraniums bloom with midsummer exuberance and the bulbs, on a snowy morning, gather in one limited spot all the essence of a fragrant April day.

CHAPTER III

IT PAYS TO SELECT THE RIGHT PLANTS

PLACING the right plant at the right window is the first step toward satisfaction. This means knowing the disposition of the kinds you admire and evaluating the light conditions you can offer them. Light and heat are the factors which determine which plants will live happily in your home.

Innumerable platitudes have been passed on from person to person about house plants. One of the most worn, and yet most true, is that flowering plants must have sunlight, foliage plants can be grown well with light alone. But that statement, to be serviceable, must be broken down into terms of specific plants.

Light But No Sunlight

What exactly would we choose if we had fully light windows but no sunlight coming in through them? Many foliage plants will thrive there. A beginner would find the following ones interesting and not too burdensome:

Aloe
Baby's Tears (*Helxine soleiroli*)
Boston Fern
Chinese Evergreen (*Aglaonema*)
Chinese Rubber Plant (*Crassula arborescens*)
Dumbcane (*Dieffenbachia*)
English Ivy
Grape Ivy
Kangaroo Vine (*Cissus antarctica*)
Nephthytis
Screw Pine (*Pandanus*)
St. Louis Ivy (*Philodendron*)
Pothos
Sedums
Snake Plant (*Sansevieria*)
Swiss Cheese Plant (*Monstera deliciosa*)
Wandering Jew (*Tradescantia*)

It might even be possible to obtain some delicate bloom from wax begonias and the periwinkle (Impatiens). After a little experience has been acquired, it would not be foolhardy to try:

Aralia
Ferns (but not the Maidenhair)
Norfolk Island Pine (*Araucaria excelsa*)
Palms

Two Hours of Sunlight

In a window perhaps east or west, through which two

or three hours of sunlight pierces, all these would be easy for the uninitiated to keep happy:

Asparagus Ferns (A. sprengeri)
Begonias
Flowering Maple (Abutilon)
House Iris (Marica)
Maranta
Osmanthus
Pick-a-Back (Tolmiea)
Peperomia
Pittosporum
Strawberry Begonia (Saxifraga sarmentosa)
Spider Plant (Anthericum)

Full Sun

Full sunlight, which is interpreted as a possible five hours a day in bright weather, makes possible fascinating excursions into indoor gardening. For in full sunlight, the flowering plants really come into their own. This means the triumphant possession of a south window. Generally speaking, however, except for geraniums and some of the begonias, none of these is as easy to grow as foliage plants. You will soon discover which ones, of the many possibilities, give you the thrill of being green-fingered.

Abutilon (Flowering Maple)
Astilbe
Azalea
Cactus

Calceolaria
Cineraria
Crown of Thorns
Gardenia
Geranium
Heliotrope
Hydrangea
Jerusalem Cherry
Kalanchoe
Lantana
Oxalis
Passion Vine
Plumbago
Poinsettia
Shrimp Plant
Sweet Olive
Hoya carnosa (Wax Plant)

Of course in this five hours minimum sunlight, practically all the varieties from the other two groups will thrive although the African violet, cyclamen and primrose are set back a little from the strong sun. If any of the others tend to wilt or yellow, they also must be protected during the hottest hour or so with a thin curtain or partially closed Venetian blind.

At this point in experience, it is possible to trust such colored foliage as coleus and the more striking varieties of Wandering Jew, perhaps the purple and silver striped Zebrina pendulosa. If you are really willing to work at this house plant business and give both thought and time to their care, these also will do well in this situation:

African Violet
Ardisia
Anthurium (Flamingo Flower)
Cape bulbs such as Freesia, Veltheimia
Cyclamen
Dutch bulbs such as Tulips, Hyacinths
Primroses

Color Month by Month

It is always important to consider not which plant is most attractive at the florist's but which plant will be healthy and therefore still attractive several months hence if grown under present available home conditions of light and sun.

Just to prove what can be done, we went through our plant diaries and picked these lists of plants which have provided us flower interest and color throughout various winters of indoor gardening. Green vines and foliage plants were always used to frame or supplement these more showy individuals.

October-November

Annuals, potted up from the garden: Ageratum, Nicotiana, Stock, Cosmos, Zinnia, Marigold

Plants: Abutilon
        African Violet
        Begonia semperflorens
        Bouvardia

Chrysanthemums
Geraniums (continued bloom from garden
    plants)
Oxalis
Plumbago capensis
Shrimp Plant
Sweet Olive (good as an alarm clock for
    Thanksgiving)

Bulbs: Lachenalia, Paperwhite Narcissus

December

Plants: African Violet
Azalea
Begonias—Wax, Christmas
Bouvardia
Christmas Cactus
Crown of Thorns
Cyclamen
Geranium
Oxalis
Passion Vine
Poinsettia
Sweet Olive

Fruit: Ardisia
Jerusalem Cherry
Peppers
Otaheite Orange

Bulbs: Narcissus, Lily-of-the-Valley, Lachenalia,
Roman Hyacinths.

January (apt to be poor in bloom because of prevailing
   cloudiness)

  Plants: African Violet
          Begonias—single and double semperflorens;
             Christmas
          Crown of Thorns
          Cyclamen
          Geranium
          Jasmine—Confederate and *J. grandiflorum*
          Marica
          Oxalis
          Poinsettia
          Primroses—*P. malacoides, obconica, sinensis
             stellata*
          Sweet Olive

  From Seed: Morning Glory
          Black-Eyed Susan Vine (*Thunbergia alata*)
          Viola

  Fruit: Ardisia
          Jerusalem Cherry

  Bulbs: Lachenalia, Lily-of-the-Valley, Paperwhite
          Narcissus, Roman Hyacinths, Veltheimia

February-March (peak months for flower production)

  Bulbs: Amaryllis, Calla Lilies, Dutch Hyacinths,
          Freesia, Lily-of-the-Valley, Narcissus,
          Ornithogalum, Tulips

Plants: African Violets
Azaleas
Begonias—semperflorens, also some species
Camellia
Crown of Thorns
Cyclamen
Gardenia
Geranium
Jasmine—Confederate and *J. grandiflorum*
Oxalis
Passion Vine
Plumbago capensis
Primroses
Roses—miniature such as Pixie, Tom
Thumb
Saxifraga sarmentosa
Spathiphyllum floribundum
Sweet Olive

Fruit: Ardisia

Forced branches: Peach, Pear, Forsythia, Lilac,
Magnolia, Flowering Crab

April

Plants: Abutilon
African Violet
Begonia semperflorens
Confederate Jasmine
Crown of Thorns
Easter Lilies

Gardenia
Geranium
Hydrangea
Oxalis
Plumbago capensis
Spathiphyllum
Sweet Olive

Seeds: Thunbergia alata

Forced branches and forced plants: Funkia, Bleeding Heart, Astilbe

May-Summer (These are nice substitutes indoors if places seem too yawningly empty after winter residents have moved to the garden. Pleasant for the porch, too.)

Achimenes
Fairy Lilies
Gloxinias
Foliage Color: Caladium

Continuous Bloom

The seasons in house plants come and go, even though their year is compressed into nine months. If gift plants for Christmas or Valentine's Day or Easter are too uncertain to count on for part of the window garden, and many of the others on these lists sound like too much work, the indoor garden has a few standbys. Yes, there is such a thing as continuous bloom. Or at least it is fairly regular bloom if light and heat are favorable. Coral Berry or Ardisia must be included in this list even though red berries from December to June may be a bit wearing. And here are the flowers:

African Violet
Begonia semperflorens
Crown of Thorns
Impatiens
Oxalis
Sweet Olive

CHAPTER IV

FIRST AIDS TO BEAUTY

ONLY the healthy house plant is decorative and only the decorative plant is worth having. Far too many specimens are sentimentally retained although their stems are leafless and their sparse foliage sickly. Apparently to all but their owners they proclaim: our day is done, we should now depart in peace. The stark rubber plant, the desperate fern, the exhausted palm, all such really belong in the crematory beyond the sight of men who, viewing them, unconsciously shudder as they pass.

This was the verdict we reached one gray January day of sleet and rain as we filled with trivial discussion tedious and fearful hours of waiting in a hospital reception room. If ever we needed color and lift, that was the day. But what did we see all around us? Only dying plants. Around the window through which we vainly sought some cheering sight, were draped yards of barren philodendron stem with but three weary yellowing leaves at the tip. The table beside us groaned beneath a ponderous, depressing aspidistra which was unfit for even a dentist's anteroom. Saddest of all were the African violets vainly struggling with the hot, dry air.

We could almost hear their gasping pleas for humidity.

Is this some grim joke, we asked, that in a spot where anxiety is inevitable, we must be companioned by dying plants? Whose idea is this, anyway, for it certainly prevails, that any plant, anywhere, in any condition is an essential delight? We take issue and repeat: *only the healthy plant is decorative.*

And here are the five basic rules which help your house plants keep their looks.

1—Let them have plenty of LIGHT for green growing, sun for flowering. No growth is possible in dark places since plants require light to manufacture food. If for decorative effect you want plants on mantel ends or in the center of the dining table, with few exceptions plan to move them to a window for many hours each day. Flowering plants vary in their sun needs from the wax begonia which blossoms, though not richly, with almost no sun at all to the geranium which requires all the direct sunlight a south window will afford. It is wise to select plant varieties with both their natures and your available conditions in mind.

2—Keep your plants on the cool side, as the florist does. The TEMPERATURE in the greenhouse is almost always many degrees below the temperature in your home. Thus the Christmas cherry thrives at 50° F. and dies at 70° F. and only a few of the tropicals can stand the winter temperatures you prefer. Even the southern gardenia is happier at 55° F. to 60° F. than at your own comfortable 70° F.

Night temperatures for house plants should also drop 5 or 10° F. as they do in nature when the sun sets. If a more pronounced decline seems likely because of exceptionally cold weather and banked night fires, then house plants need some extra protection, especially if they stand very close to the window glass. Curtains or shades may be drawn, or newspapers may be propped between glass and plants, to act as an insulating layer against below-freezing conditions.

3—A moist atmosphere is the main key to house plant success. Modern heating systems tend to dry out the atmosphere. Foliage needs to draw moisture from surrounding air. So try to coddle this want of HUMIDITY which is a basic one. Weekly refreshing of tops with water through a bulb syringe or house plant sprayer is fine; daily for the particular ones is better. The pebble saucer device or tray (page 18) or a moist fiber water mat, designed just for the purpose, are likewise excellent humidifiers.

Weekly refreshment under the fine mist of a shower bath, with plants laid on their sides to protect them from oversoaking of soil, is an event they probably look forward to all week!

With plants such as ivy, however, it is a more simple matter to keep them in exuberant health by holding them daily under the full but gentle stream of an open faucet.

The rubber plant and such smooth-leaved plants require a more careful procedure. At least once a month, they must be cleansed and refreshed by having all surfaces wiped with a clean, damp cloth. No oil must ever be added. True, it shines foliage but at the expense of the plant's basic good health.

The general humidity of a room can be improved by placing pans of water on radiators, or fastening on the radiators themselves some type of commercial humidifier. Vases of vines growing in water and strategically placed among house plants offer another source of evaporating water to moisten the air.

4—Examine plants daily. Test the feel of the soil but WATER them only when they need it. The frequency and amount depend on the weather — sunny or dull — on the pot type and size — glazed or clay, large or small — the nature of the plant — the succulent jade plant wants a little, the woodsy African violet a lot — and the stage of growth. The resting cyclamen is best left almost dry while the same plant producing leaves and buds thrives if kept quite wet. Some plants require watering once a fortnight, some twice a day.

After you have evaluated all factors, this tentative rule may help: when the top soil feels dry to the touch and when the appearance of the clay pot and the soil is light, water generously until the excess water runs into the pot saucer. Remove this extra then unless the plant is one of a very few — calla or the lovely cyclamen — which actually thrives with wet feet, or unless a pebble-filled saucer or tray can hold the overflow as a humidity reserve.

Avoid the little-and-often system of watering which moistens surface roots too frequently while the condition of the lower ones approximates the desert. With shrubby plants — azaleas and gardenias — and with large specimens of fern and palm — make certain of thorough root saturation by the SUBMERGENCE method. Once a week set each large plant, after it has gone just a little dry, in a pail or tub filled with water to within one inch of the pot brim. Let each plant remain, often a matter of hours, until enough moisture has been drawn in through the porous sides of the pot for the top soil to feel moist.

This method is also excellent for such florists' annuals as primroses and marguerites which produce flowers for months and develop much fresh green foliage as well, if for one hour out of each twenty-four, the pots are submerged in a kitchen bowl with moisture up to the pot rim. It is amazing to notice what a quantity of water each five-inch potted plant can thus absorb each morning.

Room temperature water is better than cold, and rain water preferable to that from the faucet, especially if, where you live, the water is highly chemical.

5—Remember about VENTILATION. Plants cannot step out for a breath of air each day though they need it just as much as you do. When first they are brought in in the fall, keep the windows open for long hours during the warm part of the day. This helps plants acclimate themselves to less humid indoor conditions during these first transition days and prevents excessive leaf dropping. As the weather gets colder, fresh air may have to be admitted for a few minutes daily via an open window or door in an adjoining room. Fresh air is important but cold air harmful. Always avoid chills, draughts and wind. And never set plants out in cold weather for a "refreshing shower" since they are more likely to die than be refreshed.

We are frequently asked, "Why doesn't my geranium bloom?" or "How is it that the African violets or gardenias I buy in full flower never set a bloom once their greenhouse crop is finished?"

To these direct questions on flowering failure we wish we had some simple answers. The rich blooming of plants is, however, the result of many conditions. First it is due to good general health. Second it may be dependent on some specific factor which is dictated by the original environment of the species in jungle, forest or desert.

If some cherished specimen of yours proves stubborn about budding, check first over these five basic rules of health. See if you cannot increase humidity which more often than not is the master key to the mystery. Then turn to the chapter in which we have set down our experiences with your special plant. Perhaps there you may discover some little trick of culture which for you too will spell success. We hope so, for we think flowering plants are indeed the most fun of all.

CHAPTER V

A FIRM UNDERSTANDING

NOT one of us has failed to encounter the bore who dominates a meal with a detailed catalogue of some diet. Only mutely can plants tell us of their difficulties with meat and drink by wilting if they lack water, and failing to grow if the soil is sterile. Soil and fertilizer are, however, not a panacea for every ill that a house plant can develop. But a proper soil mixture and intelligent fertilizing are the basis of good health and consequently of flourishing plants.

Soil is a topic on which it is possible to become highly technical and involved. And because the garden soil which most of us have is not usually ideally suited either in texture or nutrients to sustain a plant for several months indoors, it is natural that we feel we should try to improve it. But when it comes down to cases, we confess that 90% of our own house plants are potted and thriving in a far from fancy mixture. This is composed of the following:

2 parts good garden soil
1 part leafmold, humus or compost
1 part sharp clean sand (builder's sand, not sea sand)

For further enrichment, when plants are being potted, bone meal is added at the rate of one teaspoon for a five-inch pot. For plants that fit in smaller pots, the amount is decreased proportionately. A complete commercial fertilizer may be substituted for the bone meal.

All of these ingredients are thoroughly mixed. The pile of soil is turned with the hands until it is all one color and the sand no more distinct than the soil or humus. Then about one-third of this goodly heap of soil is sifted. The fine part is used at the top of the pot. The roughage left in the sifter is reserved for drainage at the bottom.

We admit that it is smarter to vary the component parts of this soil mixture for certain plants. For azaleas which like an acid soil, 25% peatmoss or composted oak leaves may be included in the average mixture. Cacti and succulents, which prefer a light, gritty and not very rich soil, thrive with a 25 percentage of sand and some pebbly roughage in the average soil. African violets and ferns prefer a looser, more woodsy soil. For them the amount of leafmold is increased and the sand reduced.

If you feel like experimenting with this standard mixture for ferns or begonias or any other group in which you specialize, by all means do so. But we repeat that it will nourish life a good nine months for most house plants if food is added at regular intervals.

So why harry your husband or the florist for dibs and dabs of this and that or worry about adding too much lime? House plants are hardy souls. One advantage of the soil mixture we use is that it drains well; if excess water does not make its way to the saucer underneath the plant in short order, there is something wrong with your soil mixture or method of potting.

Starting plants off in the right soil mixture is important. Once this basic principle has been settled, only a minimum of attention is needed all winter. Remember how you loosen the garden with a hoe all summer long? It isn't nearly as back-breaking to cultivate the house plants once a month. A neat little gadget with a miniature rake at one end and a spading fork at the other does the trick nicely. If you aren't fancy, an apple corer or a fork does as well. Take care that only surface soil is stirred and no fine roots broken.

Fertilize the soil, yes, but in moderation. Neither feeding nor repotting is a cure-all for sick plants. You will have to know your plants to feed them wisely. To bring this pronunciamento down to earth, only plants in active growth or approaching the flowering stage should be fed. At that once or twice a month will suffice. Too much feeding encourages soft growth.

Fertilizer left over from the summer garden should not in a burst of thrift be used up on the residents of the window garden. Plant tablets are one of the most convenient methods of feeding house plants. They may be used safely and with good results according to their manufacturer's directions. The number to be used varies with the size of the pot, and it is seldom recommended that they be applied more than once a month. The food value of a tablet is made available to the plant by pushing a pencil in the soil close to the rim of the pot (*not* the plant stem), inserting the tablet and replacing the earth. A little dissolves each time the plant is watered.

We swear too, by either Clay's fertilizer or liquid manure. A pinch of Clay's sprinkled over the soil surface of the pot and watered in works wonders. This is an imported fertilizer, not always easy to obtain, but its newer American counterpart, Electra, is also good. So does substituting liquid manure approximately once a month for tap water. Every greenhouse man has his own superlative recipe for making liquid manure. Basically it consists of steeping a bushel of horse or cow manure in a barrel of water. To it he may add varying portions of dried blood, aluminum sulphate and other rich food. Here is a good standard recipe:

> 1 quart of real cow manure
> 5 gallons of water

The manure may be suspended in a bag or simply placed in the bottom of the container. This must stand undisturbed for five weeks. At the end of this period, take one quart of this liquid and dilute it with three quarts of water for use on house plants.

It must be admitted that the use of liquid manure has its drawbacks as far as house plants are concerned, for it does have an odor hardly comparable to our favorite toilet water. If this seems disturbing, however briefly it may last, then the more modern liquid fertilizers, diluted and applied according to manufacturer's directions, are an excellent substitute.

CHAPTER VI

BASIC COMFORT

REPOTTING house plants is as inevitable as laundering the curtains. It's a day's work that faces everyone sooner or later and might just as well be done as thoroughly and managed as efficiently as the spring house cleaning. That means preparing a generous amount of soil, gathering together clean pots of all sizes, and procuring tools that will make the job progress smoothly. We usually find it easier to do this outdoors than in, so a pleasant day in spring and again in fall is likely to find us, thus surrounded, out under the grape arbor.

Pots and Pans

From the arena of experimental stations have come to our ears at various times news of a vast controversy on clay pot versus glazed or glass one. Without going into the matter very deeply we have discovered that for our simple purposes and under our average conditions plants do well in either. Practically, it settles down to the fact that watering must be more copious when clay pots are used for the simple reason that there is more evaporation through the porous sides of a clay container.

Our own choice, therefore, is largely determined by cash in hand (the lovely glazed turquoise blue, ocean green and buff containers cost a lot more than old-fashioned run-of-the-mill clay numbers) and convenience. On one thing we insist: every glazed pot must have a hole in the bottom to facilitate drainage and aeration of the soil. Often plants destined for a high shelf, a bit out of reach, are slipped into glazed pots because in those they need watering much less often.

As far as decorative values go, both types of container possess them. The simply designed, terra-cotta flower pot we all know is really pleasing in shape and substance. If a different color is preferred, it is a simple matter to give it a coat of flat oil paint in some soft blue, gray, green or yellow which will blend nicely with plants but never compete with their primary decorative interest. (Of course, after a coat of paint the pot's porosity decreases so watering is cut down for the transformed clay pot as for the glazed container.) The painting should be done before, not after, the plants are settled in their proper size pot.

Glazed pots, however, are of such charming colors and finish that we prize every one we have acquired. Vines especially are all the more attractive set in yellow or dull red containers and suspended from the wall or window frame in wrought iron scrolls or brackets. For the occasional plant which stands alone on a table, the mantel or window ledge, the glazed pot pleasingly in line with the color scheme of a room is also definitely our choice. But we never select colored glazes covered with design, since floral or geometric motifs on the pot seem unattractively competitive because of the intrinsic busy-ness of the plant forms themselves.

Our cherished and best favorite containers are those gracefully designed, pie-crust edged terra-cotta pots which come in both deep and shallow, large and small forms. Especially nice for hyacinths and tulips, azaleas and cyclamens are such beautiful bulb pans, as broad, shallow flower pots are termed.

For large clivias, camellias, and plumbago, we use, of course, wooden tubs. Our phobia and mania among containers, yes, we know we have mentioned it before, is the distorted animal form with physiognomy painfully bulged by cactus or vine. To all such cute containers, very definitely, we again say NO.

Repotting

The demon of temptation is repotting. It is easy to knock over a house plant in midwinter and break a pot just to have an excuse to do a little planting again. Don't; and don't repot just because a geranium isn't flowering or a snake plant hasn't grown six inches since October. Go over the entire group of plants once, or maybe twice, a year and repot all those that need it.

The experts will tell you that repotting should be done in May or June before the plants go outdoors for their summer vacation. Candidly, even the two of us disagree. One of us thinks it's sensible to do it when they go outdoors. The other insists it is better when they are being lifted and brought indoors since the shock of repotting in the fall does not add much to the shock of moving plants indoors and plants, on the basis of their summer growth, can be set in the right size pot for the winter performance. Spring repotting on the other hand allows plenty of time for plants to reestablish themselves in new soil, and nothing more than scrubbing the pots and a bit of trimming should be necessary in autumn.

On this point, however, we are agreed: it is better not to repot at all than to move a plant into a container which is much too large for it. Settle for a pot one size larger than the one in which the plant grew last winter. If it is not pot-bound, that is, roots are not creeping out of the drainage hole at the bottom — simply replace the old soil with fresh and reset the plant in the same pot.

There's only one way to repot, the right way. Of course, pots must be clean. Scrub the old ones with a stiff brush and soak new clay ones for hours until they have taken up all the water they will hold.

Knowing the right way to take a plant out of a pot makes you feel so professional. Slide your left hand over the top of the pot with the plant stem beneath the first and second fingers. Grasping the edge of the pot lightly, turn it upside down and tap the rim firmly against the edge of the porch steps or a table. Out should come plant, soil and all in one piece, to be neatly shifted elsewhere without roots being broken.

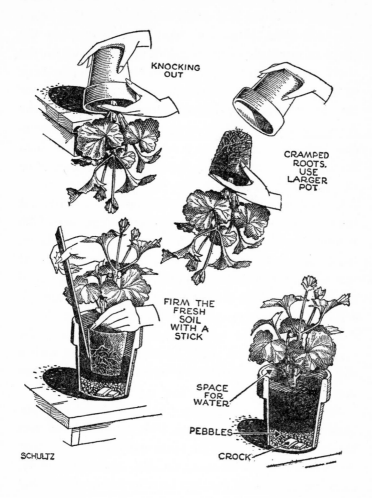

KNOCKING
OUT

CRAMPED
ROOTS.
USE
LARGER
POT

FIRM THE
FRESH
SOIL
WITH A
STICK

SPACE
FOR
WATER

PEBBLES

CROCK

SCHULTZ

A precise job of repotting comes out as smoothly as piecing a quilt block. A section of broken crock or flower pot is fitted over the drainage hole, then comes a half inch to one inch of the rough material saved from the sieve (the amount depends on the size of the pot), next a layer of the soil mixture unsifted and well firmed down with the thumbs. At this stage you'll probably want to try the plant and see how much soil needs to go beneath the roots so that it will sit at the right height.

The rest of the potting job is a two-handed affair: holding the plant in place with one hand and with the other filling in about it with soil. Save sifted soil for the top quarter of the pot. An inch-wide stick worked up and down against the sides of the pot helps to pack the soil. Tapping the bottom of the pot on a solid surface also tends to settle the soil around the plant roots.

The finished job should stand up affirmatively to three questions. Is the plant centered? Has the soil been tamped down firmly around the stem or crown of the plant so that there is no hump? Is the soil level at least one-half inch and preferably one inch below the rim of the pot?

Even the newest window gardener will find, after the first dozen plants have been repotted that these questions have been answered automatically, as they should be. When the collection of house plants grows to twenty-five or possibly a hundred, well, practice makes perfect.

CHAPTER VII

PESTS ARE NOT NECESSARY

BUGS and disease are not so inevitable with house plants as chicken pox and measles with children. They can be just as annoying if they do appear and, sneaking in on one plant, spread infectiously through the whole window garden unless stern measures are taken to circumvent them.

Many of us who have grown accustomed to cooler rooms, and healthier house plants, during heat-restricted years are almost going to forget how to control these pests. For they do thrive on heat and also on dry air. Therefore, ventilation and a weekly shower are the two most powerful preventives. A little fresh air, every day, works wonders. So, too, does the placement of each plant so that it stands alone with stems not entwined with those of its neighbors.

The weekly bath keeps foliage clean and glossy, and washes away most pests before they can obtain a foothold. Small-leaved plants such as ivies and ardisia are held under the kitchen faucet or placed beneath the bathroom shower and sprayed vigorously. The foliage of large-leaved plants such as pandanus or palms or the bulb veltheimia is cleansed with a cloth dipped in tepid, soapy water. And if African violets and others with soft leaves become dusty looking, their foliage can be freshened with a soft brush or sprayed with warm water.

But a too-warm room, a busy winter with showering neglected for a few weeks, or an infected plant inadvertently added to the window garden may introduce one of several pests. You can control any of them and get rid of most of them. But, we repeat, you can go through any winter and be bothered with not a single one.

RED SPIDER is preventable. It is annoying because the pest itself is too small to be seen by the naked eye and the unsuspecting will not know it is around until ivy leaves turn yellowish or grayish, have a fuzzy look underneath or feel crumby to the touch. Susceptible plants, especially vines, are simply kept away from sunny windows or too much heat and their weekly shower never neglected.

The cure, or more accurately, the control is pneumonia, obligingly furnished to the minute pest by spraying the upper and under sides of the foliage vigorously with cold water. If this does not clear up a persistent case, heat a pail of water to 120° F. and immerse the entire plant for thirty seconds. Thereafter, regular and hard spraying with cold water once a week should keep red spider under control.

SCALE, a larger insect, covers itself with a hard black or brown coating. It attaches itself to stems or the underside of leaves. A sucking insect, it is partial to smooth-leaved plants such as ivy, ferns and oleander, and is not to be confused with the tiny brown reproductive spores in an even pattern on the underside of fern fronds.

If the weekly shower and consequent inspection discloses only a couple of scale insects, they can be dislodged with finger nail or a toothpick and the plant sprayed once more. A heavy infestation is removed by scrubbing with an old toothbrush dipped in a strong (yellow) soap suds. Then the soaped plant stands for two hours before it is sprayed with clear, cool water.

If these remedies sound too simple a cure for so tenacious a bug, you can become involved with kerosene and soap. That is, if kerosene is at hand. It is, however, only needed for thickly infested plants which might better be thrown out anyway. If you insist on trying to save them, add a teaspoon of strong soap flakes to a quart of water. Agitate thoroughly and spray the entire plant with this mixture, leaving it on the foliage twenty-four hours before washing with clear water. Any scale treatment should be repeated at weekly intervals without fail until reappearance of the pest is doomed.

MEALY BUG consists of white cottony lumps clustered in the leaf axils of coleus, gardenia, impatiens, wax plants, even succulents and some other favorites. It thrives when plants are crowded. We have never found any better way to dispose of mealy bug than by picking off each one with a cotton tipped toothpick or matchstick dipped in alcohol or toilet water. (Frankly, a wonderful chance to use up a Christmas toilet water, whose scent is not to your liking, with good riddance to gift and pest alike.)

If you are lucky, the other three insect pests will never bother your house plants. APHIDS may appear at the leaf tips or around flower buds of some plants but they are unlikely so long as temperatures are moderate. The standard cure is nicotine sulphate in the form of Black Leaf 40, diluted with water and applied thoroughly several times, at intervals of forty-eight hours. Aphids are those tiny plant lice, either green, black or brown.

As for WHITE FLY, we learned long ago that it is best not to bring ageratum indoors in autumn for the window garden or hold over fuchsias or heliotrope. White flies love these and from them will spread to other house plants which they do not normally bother. White flies are tiny and ever so active. Spray them also with nicotine solution (Black Leaf 40), being certain to cover the underside of the foliage. Try spraying first in a warm room where the pests will be active, then for several days segregate them in a place cooler than the one they normally occupy. Repeat the spray before returning them to the usual, warmer location.

We've heard that plants are sometimes bothered with BLACK FLIES, which seem to come from the soil. The fact that our house plants have never been troubled with them is proof that not all house plants have all troubles. Since this pest does originate in the soil, we suggest replanting in a clean pot with fresh soil free of manure, and with leafmold or compost that is thoroughly decomposed. It has also been reported that black flies never bother plants kept in full sun.

THRIPS and MITE are so tiny that their presence is known only by the havoc they have wrought. Stunted growth and crumpling of leaves, sometimes limpness and yellowing are the signs. Plants so damaged are best discarded, for the only effective treatment is gas, which can be used in a greenhouse but not in a house with safety.

DISEASE SPOTS and BLIGHTS occasionally mar some plants. African violet may show ring discolorations, cacti and succulents sometimes become diseased while the leaves of certain begonias become imperfect. But these are not common nor necessarily fatal ills. The badly diseased plant, like the badly infected one, is better discarded since a complete cure is almost impossible.

The popularity of African violet leads to a wide acquaintance with ring spot. Like a favorite child with chicken pox, yellowish circles mar what should be handsome foliage. For years, this has been diagnosed authoritatively as due to careless watering from the rim of the pot so that drops of water splashed on the leaves. Sun shining directly on such plants completed the damage. Experiments conducted recently at Ohio State University indicate that spots will appear on the hairy leaf surfaces, regardless of light intensity, when the temperature of the water is lower than that of the leaf. Thus it is suggested that, if spraying is practiced, water of equal or slightly higher temperature be used. The last word on this subject has certainly not been written as yet.

CHAPTER VIII

MEET THE HOUSE PLANTS

1. The Mysterious Ways of the African Violet

LIKE the nursery rhyme child, when the African violet is good, it is very, very good but more often than not it is plain horrid. For though at its best it is as pretty a house plant as can be found, it too often stubbornly refuses to bloom again once its last greenhouse-borne bud has opened.

But what foliage then develops to tantalize an anxious owner! Healthy and green, it seems always on the verge of mass production. Next week surely it will flower, we keep thinking, until suddenly we realize that the plant has been making a fool of us for months on end. Under its present conditions it has not the slightest intention of setting a bud. Leaves, perfect leaves, are its only interest in life.

Now how can its ideals of home life be changed? What constitutes luck with African violets? It took us a long while to find out the answers and we are quite sure even now that the last word on happy home life for these saintpaulias is yet to be said. If certain fairly definite preferences are observed, we find that our African violets are almost never out of bloom, winter or summer, although at some times they are more exuberant than at others.

Saintpaulias like a comfortable warm temperature, just as we do; 70 to 72° F. is fine in the daytime and 60 to 62° at night, or even a little warmer both times. A fresh atmosphere is important and easily obtained by opening a window in an adjoining room. Stuffiness and draughts are both harmful. So is a very dry atmosphere, particularly if the heat is high. We find that wide-mouthed vases of water placed among our saintpaulias increase humidity by offering a constant source of evaporation.

Proper watering, always important for house plants, is particularly so for saintpaulias. It is absolutely essential to *use only room-temperature water*. Cold water is harmful, often causing leaf spot. Although it doesn't matter whether plants are watered from the top or the saucer, it's more convenient from below because of the spreading leaves. We pour into the saucers each morning just enough water as will be absorbed by *early* afternoon — and, of course, we had to observe for some time just how much this would be; otherwise we emptied out any excess about two o'clock. We also spray our plants about once a week with *room-temperature* water to remove dust and stimulate bloom. Plants are then kept out of the sunshine until the foliage dries.

We avoid root nematodes by sterilizing the soil for saintpaulias. We soak each potful with boiling water.

When it dries, we stir it well, water it once, and let it dry to a workable consistency, and then plant. To deter mites — much easier than getting rid of the invisible terrors — we spray once a week or so with Optox or N.N.O.R. Our attitude toward strange saintpaulias is entirely unfriendly. To avoid contaminating our cherished plants, we keep all unknowns at a distance for a two months' trial period. During that time we use a separate pitcher for watering them and wash our hands before going near our other plants. If then they look healthy, have no undue thickening, curling, or hairiness, we spread the welcome mat!

Saintpaulias are friendly plants we've found. In fact, our interest in them has resulted in some delightful new friendships and we can't help suggesting to everyone interested to join the African Violet Society of America, Inc. (Box 901, Alexandria, Virginia) so you can correspond with other "violet-crazy" people and perhaps exchange leaves with them to extend your collection. It's so easy to start new plants with a few such gifts. We just cut fairly mature leaves and insert the leaf stems about half way down in a shallow dish filled with stones and water. In about two weeks leaves of Ionantha start rooting. (Some of the du Ponts act more slowly.) A week or so later a small green leaf may push out at the base of the parent leaf. Soon a whole cluster of leaves develops. If the parent leaf remains firm and healthy, we let it stay until the new leaves are about one inch long. (Then we sometimes use the parent leaf, its stem shortened, a second or even a third time. One leaf of Big Boy produced three crops of fourteen, twelve, and six, respectively!)

If the parent leaf looks unfit we discard it at any time after the first new leaf appears. Then we immediately transfer the young plants to three-inch pots of light soil. (Soil scraped from underneath a shrub is nice and humusy.) In less than five months the new saintpaulia is well-developed and there are flowers before its first birthday, often at nine months. And incidentally, a friend who has grown them from seed finds that blooming plants develop in less than a year too!

Don't be discouraged if some of the leaves you have put in water don't seem to do much for awhile. They're probably just making up their minds. So long as they are firm and upright, they are healthy.

The leaves travel well, particularly in cool weather, if the leaf stem is wrapped in damp peat moss, then the leaf itself enfolded in facial tissue, and the whole encased in waxed paper and boxed so that it will not move around during the journey.

Saintpaulias combine beautifully with wax begonias, such as Pink Pearl, with grape ivy, the rabbit's foot fern (*Davallia lucida*) and with other house plants, but the African violet collector, of whom there are thousands today, cares little for such minor decorative triumphs and rarely combines her treasures with other house plants. She strives instead for windows filled with a representative collection — singles, doubles, variegateds, bicolors, miniatures, and oddities of hanging-basket or Blue Chard type.

Although it is possible to have perhaps a hundred different "violets," we think a window looks pretty nice if it includes the full color range represented by Bicolor, Blue Boy, Blue Eyes, Blue Girl, Blushing Maiden, Double Blue Boy, du Pont Lavender Pink, Mentor Boy, Orchid Beauty, Orchid Flute, Pink Beauty, White Lady.

Through the winter African violets do best in east windows but when the sun gets hot there in late spring or early summer, they are moved to a light, cool, sunless northern location. There the windows are open frequently for long periods to let in the pleasing humidity of the out-of-doors and there all through the hot months the saintpaulias seem never to need a rest but keep producing one bright lovely spray after another. A protected open porch is also a good vacation spot.

2. The Amaryllis Is Certain to Please

THE amaryllis is the darling of both amateur and professional, cherished by the one for its easy, spectacular beauty and by the other for its fascinating hybridizing possibilities.

For this is a tropical traveler that rarely fails to produce in the grand manner, each bulb thrusting up one or more sturdy stalks bearing three to six giant blooms which are pure white, candy cane striped, velvet red or salmon pink. Because of the size of the lily-like blooms — they may measure ten inches across — and the barbaric brilliance of many of the varieties, the amaryllis must be thoughtfully selected to harmonize with the color scheme of the rooms it will adorn. Otherwise the clash can be terrific.

On the market from November until April, the bulbs usually require at least six weeks for thorough root development, though sometimes longer, and then three or four more weeks to perfect the flowers. If these do not appear and only a disappointing amount of leaf growth develops, the amaryllis can usually claim one of two alibis — it has been planted too deeply or else has

been given such an oversize pot that all its energies have gone to filling the container with roots. It has not had strength to give a thought about flowering.

The best plan is to use pots which are only one or two inches larger than the diameter of the bulbs themselves. Usually the six-inch size is right. Rarely is anything above the seven-inch needed. In each pot is first placed an adequate layer of coarse drainage material, about one and one-half inches of broken crock with some small stones above this, or all of it of coarse gravel. A layer of rich garden soil plus a teaspoon of bone meal goes on top of this. Now the bulb is set high enough so that neck and shoulders rest above the top level of the soil. This means leaving uncovered one-half to one-third of the bulb, a most necessary precaution.

Potting firmly finished, the amaryllis is well watered and set away to get about root making in a dark cool place, at about 50° F. During the ensuing six to eight weeks little watering is required, about once in seven to ten days or less will suffice.

As soon as rooting is satisfactorily completed, the plant will push forth a flower bud. When this appears the amaryllis is no longer a cellar plant but one for the window. First place it in the light until it greens up after its dark sojourn and then move it to full sun. Be sparing with water, until the flower stalk is about four inches long, then, much more generous as the plant indicates a greater and greater capacity for absorbing moisture. Once a fortnight apply a half cup of weak liquid manure when you water it.

For its flower-producing period, a sunny east window is ideal and there it is best if the temperature does not rise above 70° F. Indeed, nearer 60° F. is much better. A too dry atmosphere is also to be avoided.

You can count on one flower stalk for every four leaves but the leaves will not make much of an appearance until the flowers are faded. Then after the big flowering stalk is cut away, a fine green strap-leaved plant will adorn your window. This must be cared for as faithfully as when it was in flower for it is now and through the summer, after it is plunged in the semi-shaded garden, that the amaryllis will be developing the embryo blooms which you are counting on for next year.

Therefore, keep up the extra feeding until late in August. The plant stays outdoors but is only lightly watered thereafter, until the first light frost. Then it is brought indoors, kept dry until the foliage is loose and can be removed, when it is ready for storage in a dark cool place. Watering it about once in three weeks or even less is sufficient during this early winter rest.

Have in mind to examine the plant occasionally from November on, although signs of growth are not likely until January. When the green point appears, scrape away what you conveniently can of the top soil and renew with some fresh mixture (you will always have a box of it saved for such winter emergencies if you are an enthusiast) plus bone meal.

Practically never is the amaryllis to be disturbed by repotting. Let it first actually break its container with the force and size of its root system. Then simply un-mold the broken segments of the old pot from the root ball and slip the plant almost untouched by human hands into the next size pot.

The amaryllis is a plant not for a day, not for a week, not for a year — (well you know that ad too). Actually it does stay by you pretty nearly forever. In time it will slowly form some new bulbs but don't be too anxious to deal with these. They must stay near the parent until they separate very easily.

Patient indoor gardeners (which we confess we are not, preferring grand good looks in a plant to labored horticultural investigation) could have an interesting time with amaryllis seed which is slow but worthwhile if a whole crop is wanted.

However, if you, like us, are in the one- or two-bulb class, consider a handsome (and expensive) white variety. Queen Elizabeth is a scarce beauty, but the Dutch Hybrid, Royal Pure White, is at hand and would make a very nice Christmas present for you to give to yourself!

3. Azaleas Have Elegance

FORTUNATE indeed is the recipient of an azalea, for she is "twice blessed": with an incomparable gift plant and a permanent addition to her indoor or outdoor garden. Whether it be Christmas, Easter or Mother's Day, azaleas are plentiful and tempting. Our recourse in deciding among the snowy white, flaming rose, or one of the melting pink shades assumed by the myriad blossoms on this trim and shapely little shrub is the eeny-meeny-miny-moe method. Luckily, true reds do not exist to complicate matters.

Two general classes of azaleas are sold in the florist shops. Either one has a future in the window garden but if preferred, one sort may have its future in the outdoor garden. Although the decision is not as weighty as selecting a college for your daughter, nevertheless it is well to know which is which.

As a general rule, the indoor or house azalea (usually A. *indica*) bears an uncanny resemblance to a small tree. It has a miniature trunk, quite barky, and its small branches form a rounded crown. The flowers are comparatively large. Glistening white, pale pink, true rose and white-flecked pink are variations equally handsome and showy.

The other azalea sold as a gift plant is the hardy or semi-hardy outdoor sort so often forced for winter bloom. Instead of the single well-developed trunk of the tender kind, this hardy type starts branching low and close to the base of the plant. The stems, also woody and hardened, are fairly slender and the evergreen leaves smaller. Nothing could be more appealing than a small plant hardly larger than a rooted cutting, fairly smothered with delicate pink blossoms. Pink shades range from soft to vivid, and there is another lovely white. The hardy Hinodegiri type with its masses of flame color bloom has formerly been predominant at Easter time but recently the semi-hardy Kurume azaleas have come more into favor. Snow, Coral Bell and Pink Pearl are deservedly popular.

Whichever type you fall heir to, a single plant will have no trouble holding its own from a decorative standpoint, wherever it is placed indoors. The azalea deserves a restrained setting, however, without competition from other flowers since it makes window garden, window sill, bookcase or desk (if touched by sun) a focus of attention for weeks and weeks. A multitude of buds attends to that.

Three things azaleas ask to maintain perfection: sun in moderation, a temperature between the 50-60° F. range rather than a sustained 65° F. or higher, and water in abundance. An east or west window is the perfect location for a flowering plant. Our plant stands in the deep saucer which, filled with water in the morning, is always empty at night. (A mass of small roots which drink thirstily support the azalea.)

Like the gardenia, the azalea flourishes if once a week it is allowed to become fairly dry and the pot is then immersed in a pail filled with water to within an inch of the pot rim. Here the plant remains until the soil has taken up all the moisture it can hold.

So that nothing will mar the prospective three months of bloom, the final detail is nipping off faded blossoms. Coolness and moisture do the rest.

In May, the azalea's future must be decided. If the hardy type is to graduate to the garden, it is transplanted in the customary manner. If either the treelike Indica or the hardy kinds are to carry on their tradition as house plants, they must be repotted in fresh soil and plunged in a partially shaded garden spot until September. A two-inch layer of ashes or small pebbles beneath the pot will facilitate drainage, keep worms from entering and ease lifting in autumn because roots will not have worked their way through the hole in the pot into the soil.

The azalea prefers an acid soil mixture, and while vacationing outdoors, some fertilizing. Two or three applications of liquid manure at intervals of six weeks help the plant to store up energy for winter bloom. Considerable watering especially during a prolonged drought is also necessary. This plant cannot be forgotten during summer.

Before frost the azalea is lifted and brought indoors. Fall is really the dormant period so plants at this time are not fed, and will need less water than when they are in flower (although they should never be allowed to dry out). Light and coolness are their immediate needs. A temperature of 50° F. and a north window are favorable. When November comes, azaleas are transferred into warmer and fully light quarters such as a south window. Feeding with liquid manure is resumed on a weekly schedule. During all of this period, the plants are syringed regularly with cold water, for they are susceptible to red spider. As soon as flower buds commence to open, showering must cease for it is difficult to spray foliage without spotting the blossoms.

The miracle (hardly that after catering to their growth routine) occurs in early December when flower buds appear. As soon as a few have opened, back go the plants to an east or west window so that each blossom may be enjoyed for the longest possible time. North, south, then east or west, that is the compass for the azaleas' residence from September to May and in following it, the window gardener enjoys each year a recurring glory from this gift plant.

4. All Begonias Are Beauteous

THE everblooming wax begonia *(Begonia semperflorens)* is as valuable in the window garden as the good little black dress in a woman's wardrobe. Rarely does a winter pass that we do not feature this beauteous little plant, especially since we have discovered that excellent larger flowering trio of varieties — White, Pink, and Red Pearl.

Because of their pleasing appearance and good dispositions these wax begonias are probably the best of all winter-flowering house plants. Amenable to either light or sunny locations, resistant to pest and disease, they flower freely from October to June, provided they are pinched back enough to keep them stocky and branching, and provided also that they are neither overwatered nor allowed to stand in water.

For some reason, perhaps their succulent look, these begonias seem to invite overwatering. Yet that is the very condition these tolerant plants cannot endure. If permitted to dry out well between drinks and if the foliage is lightly cleansed by syringing once a month, the wax begonias inevitably thrive. Indeed, though there are more spectacular flowering indoor plants not one is more regularly dependable.

We know that now we sound just like a catalogue description and we do apologize but the point is whenever anyone swims into our ken who isn't wax-begonia-wise, we always go on like this. We can't bear the thought of so many frustrated indoor gardeners struggling with gardenias, when all they need for complete satisfaction is a nice row of always in-bloom wax begonias.

And decoratively they have so many possibilities, especially in east windows. Possibly we enjoyed ours most the year we grew pink and white ones in an otherwise green window of English and grape ivy and philodendron, with our china kitten collection as accessories after the constant fact of their flowering. For it seemed that the kittens and the wax begonias were ideal companions. Why, we couldn't quite say. Perhaps there is a certain winsome or puckish quality about them both. White begonias with red poinsettias and pink begonias with purple African violets have been delights of other years.

These wax begonias have a double flowering variety, too, and the day a New England cousin gave us several slips of hers remained a highlight of that summer holiday. If single begonias are winsome, the doubles are utterly captivating. Blossoms are like the tiniest of rose buds in little-girl pink and almost cover the plant. The doubles root as easily in water as the singles but they are more difficult to grow well, for thrips appear without apparent provocation if the plants spend the winter in a warm room. During fall and early winter they are quiescent but the rest of the year flower abundantly.

It is easy, too, to keep a big wax begonia supply available with no money changing hands after the original investment. Getting them started from seed is far from arduous, while May-made cuttings appear eager to bloom by July (we discourage such exuberance by much pinching back until late September). Or older plants may be held over. They are simply cut back hard, in fact, within an inch or so of their lives, at the time of the outdoor transfer. Then they are repotted in containers one size larger and grown through the summer on the porch or under a tree, where moderate shade and shelter from wind are assured.

The soil for begonias must be light and porous (with an extra proportion of leafmold) so as to be easily penetrated by fine roots. Careful and adequate drainage arrangement in the pot is also important.

Besides these smaller treasures there are many large, almost tree-like species which produce in winter and spring truly handsome panicles, often lacy in form, of pink, white or rose bloom. Just for a starter we suggest six kinds which over a period of years have been easy for us to grow under the most average conditions and yet have given us much pleasure first, because of their contrasting leaf forms and then because of their blossoms. (We do not recommend the Rex type since they are mostly on the dormant side during the winter nor the controversial calla begonia which is too temperamental for our taste, though a joy to those who can manage it.)

Begonia corallina lucerna has the largest flowers of all, bearing great pendent clusters of deep pink to red blooms on plants that readily reach twenty-four to thirty inches and could go much higher. Leaves are dark green, broad at the base, long and pointed. We find this one loves a south window.

Then there are two ill-named "beefsteak" begonias

with thick round shiny leaves, much more like water lily pads than beefsteak. Procumbent in foliage habit, these bear light pink sprays of color held high above the foliage and appearing in gala processions from January to July. For baskets, where a mound of leaves looks well this *Begonia feastii* and the ruffled and crested form of it, *B. bunchii*, are unkillable and most attractive.

B. haageana is a shrubby upright type with white-tinted pink hanging blooms. One of the sturdiest of all, it bears flowers which look like purses. They are conveniently winter rather than spring-appearing.

B. heracleifolia is a Mexican variety of the lovely star type with a long January to March display of rose colored loveliness. Even at a northeast window it is of constant color.

B. Verschaffeltiana we have been fond of for years and we grow it, of all places, on one of those old-fashioned kerosene lamp brackets fastened to the bathroom window frame. This common rhizomatous type, we are sure, has never let anybody down. The light pink airy clouds of bloom keep rising from the sturdy, red-tinted hairy leaves for a long and luscious season, usually from January to March.

Besides these six "easies" we have had a fair success with that vine-like gem, *B. glaucophylla scandens*, which is far more humidity-dependent than the others and completely intolerant of extreme heat in summer. And when we get a gift plant of the handsome bulbous Christmas or Melior Begonia we also cherish this for a time, considerately growing it on till it goes dormant in late winter. Then it is left completely dry and cool in the cellar until May, when it is laid outside beside the cyclamen and, like it, repotted in August. In growth, the meliors need quantities of water from the saucer and glaucophylla also is better if always barely moist.

Our favorite six like the wax type do well if dried off a bit between drinks. All are readily propagated from leaf cuttings (see page 180 for method) and in summer their brittle growth is but lightly pruned back. The plants are kept well out of wind on the porch.

Begonias generally are very fond of humidity and dependent on fresh air too. A temperature between 60° F. and 70° F. is pleasing and not too deep planting essential. If set with a barely rising crown they are happier than when placed in a depression where water may collect.

For ease of culture, dependability of bloom and variety of foliage, you cannot really find an equal to the begonia. And because there are some five hundred very handsome varieties you may enjoy collecting them. You will discover there are many other enthusiasts who take their begonias quite seriously, exchanging round robin letters of experiences, many even joining societies to grow and talk about their plants. Like geranium and ivy collecting, begonias can become a most fascinating hobby.

5. Preview of Spring with Bulbs

WHEN February blizzards rage, an authentic touch of spring burgeons in the window garden. For it is then that daffodils, tulips and hyacinths begin to flower indoors. If you are not the energetic type who saves a few bulbs from those being planted outdoors in October to be potted for indoor enjoyment, the florist will come to the rescue with well-timed and superbly forced pans of these bright beauties.

Daffodils or narcissi are the sprightliest as well as the easiest to bring into perfect advance flowering. The good old King Alfred daffodil is the standard florist variety, but we gardeners who do not have to consider market preferences may attempt any of the legion of Narcissus types and varieties, which we plant in the garden. Tulips are handsome for the brief time we enjoy their flowers but save for the single and double early types, they are most undependable for winter bloom, especially when undertaken by the amateur. Any of the hyacinths are delightful and worth while — either the fat, sweet-scented Dutch type, the more slender Roman hyacinth or the perky little grape hyacinth that brings a bit of sky indoors.

As a matter of fact, grape hyacinths are the simplest of all. Plant a few in a pot of any good garden soil in October and keep it in a cool place, not too inaccessible for twice-a-week watering until the foliage sprouts. Then, if they are moved into a sunny window, the first week of February invariably discloses tiny blue cones of buds pushing up into the light. We enjoy both the flowers and the simplicity of obtaining them.

We have been curious as to how many indoor gardeners bother now-a-days with the routine of forcing the other hardy bulbs. Probably more than there should be in view of the exacting conditions that must be maintained to assure winter bloom. If you want to try it, the directions sound simple enough but the coolness and the darkness and the timing requisite to success must be maintained no matter how great the nuisance.

A soil mixture rather on the sandy side is favorable not only for flowering but for the complete maturity of these hardy bulbs so that they will be worth planting in the garden next fall. Two parts of garden soil, one part leafmold or humus and two parts sand will stimulate good growth. A better showing is made if these bulbs are planted in pans which are wide enough to permit three hyacinths or daffodils or four to six tulips per 6-inch pan. Tulip bulbs are set so that their noses are just below the surface of the soil (which as always is one inch below the rim of the pot), narcissus bulbs level with the soil surface, and hyacinths barely peeking out.

This group of bulbs insists on darkness and a cold temperature while roots grow. They can be set outdoors in a coldframe or arranged in a pit or trench dug for them and covered with ashes, burlap or heavy paper. They will need to be mulched heavily so that they do not freeze and can be lifted in January with some degree of ease. It is largely a matter of intuition when these pans of bulbs can be moved indoors. However, October-potted ones should have made sufficient root growth to be ready for the transfer during the first week in January. A light and cool place indoors is the next resting place, then as top growth develops, more light and a higher temperature (50-55° F.). When flower buds show, they can be given full sun and warmth.

During all of this period, watering is necessary. The pans should be soaked right after planting and be watered at least once a week while they are in cold storage. When they are brought indoors, watering is stepped up to three times a week or as often as is necessary for steady growth.

Honestly, we think all this is a lot of bother and the game not worth the candle. Certainly it is hardly worthwhile when facilities are limited and the florist can provide so readily the few pans of bulbs which satisfy our heart's desire. As for trying spring crocus and snowdrop — well, we have in the dim past and consider it a waste of time. The trick with crocus, so we have heard, is to start them late and grow them cool. Certainly this is worth a trial, if you can't wait for the first yellow ones to pop out in the garden in March but November planted crocus are inevitably slow and disappointing indoors.

It is the height of foolishness to regard your private and advance spring, no matter what its source, as the end of this bulb story. These hardy bulbs have a prolonged future outdoors if they are not relegated to the back porch or cellar the day their blooms fade. They pay rich dividends in return for a few more weeks of the intelligent and regular attention given to the other house plants. The dead flowers, of course, are cut off but the plants are allowed to stay in an east or west window. There they are watered as needed until the yellowing leaves indicate the bulbs have matured and are about to enter their resting period. At this stage the pans are stored in a cool dry place. Some day in spring, the bulbs can be shaken free of soil and saved for the fall session of bulb planting in the garden. In two years time, they will flower as freely as though they had never been seen in a window garden.

6. Mixed Blessings in Minor Bulbs

BITS of color, a procession of bloom and the fun of experiment await the window gardener who is willing to try some of the lesser known bulbs and corms which are listed in the fall catalogues. You probably won't want to attempt all of the possibilities every year and you won't be entirely successful (measuring success in terms of snakeplant, wax begonias or paperwhite narcissus) with some of them. But until a gamble has been taken, it is only human to wonder how they will perform.

Autumn crocus, for example, is charming one year but unexciting several years in a row. Nothing is easier or quicker to bring into flower than this *Crocus sativus*. As soon as the bulbs are procurable in early fall, they may be planted in sandy soil or in a pebble-filled saucer. No storage period is necessary. Before you know it the delicate spring-like crocus blossom has unfolded, utterly alone in its fragile white or lilac beauty, for foliage does not appear until the flower has faded.

Two of the easiest bulbs to bring into bloom in the

window are the South African immigrées Lachenalia or
Cape Cowslip and Veltheimia. Growing them is an easy
matter, for they are simply planted in pots of soil during
October, placed at once in an east or west window and
watered regularly. Foliage appears promptly and bloom
is certain to follow.

Lachenalia, planted in October (three bulbs to a
four-inch pot) display in December short spikes clustered with rose or red blossoms. Veltheimia is a large
bulb, resembling the amaryllis, and, like it, is potted half
in and half out of the regular soil mixture. The veltheimia needs a large container however, for it develops
into a handsome spreading foliage plant long before it
flowers. A six-inch pot is the minimum both for roots
and good balance of top growth.

We sometimes wonder if we don't enjoy veltheimia
fully as much as a foliage plant. The broad, shiny and
brilliant green leaves grow in rosette fashion and make a
truly handsome plant. The flower bud will show by New
Year's at the latest and slowly push more than a foot
above the rosette of foliage to open many small rose
colored blossoms, sometimes tinted with yellow or
green. Flowers from both of these bulbs last at least six
weeks provided they are kept out of strong sunlight. If,
when they have withered, they are cut off and the plant
watered twice a week until foliage has matured, the
bulbs can be saved for planting another year.

The Peruvian Daffodil, so prompt and dependable in
the summer garden, is also a winter possibility. Perhaps
you know it as spider lily or basket flower. Whatever

the name, fragrant white blooms are curiously like winged lilies. Eight weeks are needed to produce flowers and if you wish to use those bulbs which blossomed previously in the garden, they need a three-months rest before being put to work again. The method of potting, soil and care after blooming is identical to that given amaryllis.

From these bulbs we progress to others which are less dependable for flower results but worth a whirl some winter if only to say "I told you so". Two of these candidates are Gladioli and Ornithogalum. You can, if you wish, grow a few of the large-flowered varieties of gladioli, if they have been especially treated for forcing. The white Maid of Orleans or violet Pelegrina, yellow Loyalty or pink Los Angeles are window garden subjects. More delightful are the small flowered *Gladiolus nanus* or the fragrant *Gladiolus tristis*. To be safe plant in January for April bloom, covering bulbs with two inches of soil and setting them two inches apart. They need no rest period and come along rapidly in a temperature of 50 to 60° F.

Ornithogalum have been for us a snare and a delusion but they are lovely if you can work magic on them. The forcing kinds are a far cry from the prolific little garden Star of Bethlehem. One variety, arabicum, has clusters of small white flowers with a black center; saundersi bears pure white blossoms. Both are produced on tall stems, and perhaps are even nicer for cutting than as potted plants.

Their culture is similar to that of freesias which we

also consider skittish. Slow forcing seems to be the secret with all of them. They must be started early, meaning August or September. A soil mixture consisting of two parts garden loam, one part leafmold, one part manure and one part sand will help matters along. The pots occupy a coldframe where they can be shaded until frost threatens. The cellar or a cool room is the next resting place until roots show through the drainage hole of the pot. A light but still cool room is the next move and then if you have watered correctly, flower buds should appear during January. Of course, after the bulbs have been planted, the pots are soaked, moderate watering follows and is increased to daily watering when top growth appears. This is broken by liquid manure once a week when buds show.

Freesias are said to like warm days, cool nights and light shade. Whether they flower or not, they require staking. But unless one can be certain of midwinter flowers, are either freesias or ornithogalum worth all the fuss? Try them once, though, for the molten gold or delicate pastels of freesia and the striking white of ornithogalum are a goal worthy of achievement.

To this list of question marks, we must in fairness add bletilla, brodiaea, calochortus, sparaxis and leucocoryne. They are, for the most part, grown along in the manner of freesia. If a warm unventilated closet is your idea of a dark place, or 65 to 70° F. of a cool room, these bulbs are licked before they start — and veltheimia or lachenalia the limit of your discoveries.

7. Narcissus and Other Bulbs on a Water Diet

BULBS which can conveniently subsist on a water diet alone are a delight to all busy people today who have lots of other essential things to tend to besides flowers. Once the packaged pebbles and the bulbs are secured — and bargain collections are definitely out, only first rate, top size large or "jumbo" ones being sufficiently trustworthy — planting is a simple matter.

We time our paperwhite or polyanthus narcissus blooms first for Thanksgiving. Sometimes an earlier crop can be obtained but as a rule plantings made much before early October are not likely to turn out very well. Our fall plantings require about two weeks to produce flowers after the roots are formed, which consumes about three weeks. The nearer planting comes to their natural outdoor flowering time in early spring, the shorter is the time for developing so that March plantings often take but fourteen to twenty-one days to flower.

We always order in September about two dozen bulbs. After spreading them out for further ripening on a cool sunny window sill, we mark on a calendar the times for planting, saving at least two sets of threes for the Easter window, if we possibly can. Sometimes this is difficult because bulbs are so insistent on sprouting. Storing them in open bags in a dry, airy pantry that is definitely cold, though not freezing, seems to hold them back safely and conveniently.

All kinds of decorative effects are possible with narcissus since attractive and colorful containers are at hand in every woman's own vase and bowl department. We use oblong white bowls in pairs for balance in the window garden, a round leaf green bowl for the dining table and a Chinese rose oval for occasional use in the study. As conversation pieces for a special luncheon party we plant separate narcissus bulbs in blue-handled crystal beer mugs or sparkling amber ice tea glasses.

Filled one-third to one-half with pebbles the mugs and tumblers look charming when each carries a fragrant paperwhite narcissus in bloom. With one set at each guest's place, the table looks sprightly and gay. This effect, of course, is dependent on fine bulbs and experienced timing.

The important thing with all plantings is that containers be deep enough, that is four or five inches, so that enough pebbles can be spread under and around them to give adequate support to the big root masses which develop. Short stocky growth, sturdily upright, is the aim. Proper culture enters into this result, of course, as well as deep setting.

At planting time, bulbs in odd threes, fives or sevens are arranged fairly close together but not touching either each other or the sides of the container. Two inches of pebbles are spread beneath them and enough around them to permit only the sprouting points to be exposed. Five bulbs to a twelve-inch bowl is the proper allowance unless the bulbs are unusually large. A lump of charcoal keeps the water sweet.

After the planting is made, enough water is added to reach the base of the bulbs but not enough to cover or float them, a condition resulting in rot. More is added as evaporation takes place. For some weeks bowls are set in a dark or dim place where the temperature is around 60° F. or even less. Then they are brought to the light but not to greater heat, and flowers form just before Thanksgiving. Bright sun is avoided until the buds are well developed and as soon as flowers are open, the plants are again set out of it to prolong freshness.

Grown cool, narcissus bulbs produce good flowers without overhigh lush foliage. Draughts or nearness to radiator heat are the causes of blasted buds and spindly, lush growth, which flops over the edges of the containers and presents a far from finished looking final effect. Once these bulbs have bloomed they are discarded.

*   *   *   *   *

Other highly satisfactory pebble and water plants are the lovely creamy white and yellow Chinese sacred lilies or joss flowers and the Soleil d'Or or Golden Sun narcissus, both a little slower to grow than the polyanthus narcissus. If forced toward spring they make a most pleasing green and yellow harmony for a window garden, in combination with vases of short forsythia branches also forced to flower ahead of outdoor schedule.

Then there are two kinds of hyacinths, the Dutch, familiar to us in outside gardens and the relatively unknown tender French Roman with graceful nodding bells not so compactly placed on stems that are shorter too. Few indoor gardeners seem to have tried these French Roman charmers which we for a decade anyway have prized for the window garden pageant at Christmas. In white or porcelain blue, they may be set alone or arranged in containers with pieces of rooted philodendron or ivy inserted among the pebbles at the edges of the bowls.

The French Roman hyacinths require an eight-week period of dark, cold growing in which to develop their roots and then three to four weeks more for top perfecting. Thus bulbs can be planted early in September and brought to sun and warmth (not above 65° F. though) about November first. For Christmas, bulbs are planted early in October and forced about December first.

Single Dutch varieties are nice to rely on for the late winter picture and best not forced until the end of

January. They do well either in special hyacinth glasses or in bowls with pebbles but ten to twelve rooting weeks are essential and then about a month for further development of the tops.

Daffodils though rarely tried also are amenable to aquatic life. In the autumn you can dig up a few of your own bulbs, and store them until late January in a cool, dry place indoors. Temperatures of 50° F. or a little less give the best results. Or for this water cure you can buy short cupped varieties such as Conspicuus, Firebrand and White Lady and have a lot of fun making them behave in the way you have expected only the familiar narcissus to do.

Select some attractive container. A footed, turquoise-blue pottery bowl made a lovely color contrast one year for our golden experiment. In it we placed the bulbs in their nest of pebbles with a few bits of charcoal for permanent sweetness and enough water to maintain a level just touching the base.

After planting, set your bulbs away in a dark spot for two weeks for 60° F. growing. If the flower spike is well out of the bulb before that time, consider the preliminary rooting stage accomplished. Then bring the bowls or vases to the living room where in a fairly bright, not too warm window you should have flowers in another two weeks. As a rule thirty days after planting is a good allowance especially if you have taken pains to procure first quality stock for your experiment.

Most of these pebble and water obligers are discarded once their flowering days are past, except perhaps the

Dutch hyacinths and the daffodils which so often have a future if planted outside in spring in a sunny garden bed. This indoor forcing, however, has been hard on all of them. They bloom well for us because under field conditions they "have each stored away a blossom." In pebbles and water, lacking nutrients, they cannot store and furthermore, many are tender bulbs not winter hardy in our outdoor gardens.

8. The Christmas Cactus for Christmas Cheer

THE cactus plant we have long treasured comes not from the desert but from the mountains of Brazil where, like the orchid, it grows on the branches of trees. This is the Christmas or crab cactus (*Epiphyllum truncatum*) a constant beauty which blooms almost before its slip days are over and continues each year to grow in grace, dignity and floriferousness. In December or January it regularly puts on a show to challenge every other denizen of the window garden with some two dozen fuchsia-like flowers dripping from all the leaf tips which cover the five-inch pot. We are told that a really ancient plant may produce hundreds of blooms and our own experience makes this seem quite believable hearsay.

Unlike the desert types, this Christmas flowering beauty is the better for a soil containing plenty of both leafmold and sand. It takes rather careful handling if the buds are to appear and develop freely. These are also shown to better advantage if the plant is firmly staked so that in maturity the growth develops in fountain form but lifted somewhat above the soil level of the pot. To make the most of this graceful type of growth, florists often graft this zygocactus on some stronger cactus stem stock. Then a standard or tree form develops which is extremely attractive and necessarily a bit expensive. We consider our own ungrafted Christmas cactus, however, as the bracket plant par excellence when in maturity its long arms of growth trail over the sides of its container and every leaf tip is lit with bloom.

This is a plant which like a weary child never wants to rest, so you must be the one to determine bed time and yourself draw the shade. We get the best of blooms on ours by arranging an absolute sleeping period through the entire month of October when the plant is set in a dim cool place and watered not a single drop. In November then we water it a little and by the end of the month move it to the window garden, at first back a little from the sun but soon fully in it.

When fresh new tip growth indicates the Christmas cactus is again fully awake, we water it at first weekly, then, as growth increases, about every other day, never more and sometimes rather less, depending on the brightness of the weather. As the buds form, watering is always checked a little because a too-wet condition loosens them. About a half cup of weak liquid manure is given every ten days from the time growth is well started after the rest period until the buds show color. This means from about December first until near Christmas or maybe January if budding is late. After flowering is over, watering is again decreased. (If by chance you should overwater it and so cause limp growth and discolored tips, you can rejuvenate your plant by cutting back to firm growth.)

Repotting is a rare necessity since close compacting of soil and roots stimulates blooming and extra food needs are tended to yearly by the manure doses. When a larger pot is required, however, the shift is made in late spring just before the cactus is placed on another bracket, out of the wind on the shaded porch.

New plants can be readily started then too, from old arms of growth containing new tips. Cuts are made at the joints where small aerial roots are already in evidence. The new plants soon take hold in small pots of the regular soil. These youngsters have often bloomed for us their first Christmas.

9. Desert Cacti for the Untoward Window

As TRULY American as an ice cream soda or the Fourth of July is that whole entrancing plant group we call the cacti. The old world boasts not a single species but in the new, especially in the southwestern United States and Mexico, there are innumerable kinds flourishing under the most unlikely conditions of plant growth while bearing bizarre and amazing blooms. These do not arise conservatively on stems like most of the flowers we know, but they appear suddenly without transition, right from the top or side of the sphere or cone or cylinder which constitutes the cactus plant itself.

Beautiful and richly hued as the cactus blooms are,

however, it is not so much on their account that cacti are grown in window gardens. For the blooms are a variable matter. Sometimes in spring mature plants produce glowing color but more often they do not. It is their extremely diverse forms which make these native plants so decoratively useful. Their descriptive nicknames suggest the possibilities — the barrel cactus, bishop's cup, star, strawberry, dumpling, pincushion, hedge hog, old man (and it has white hair too) prickly pear and Turk's cap.

To the Mexican colors and furnishings of a game room and to modern architecture and modern furnishings, cacti have a special affinity, and also we must add, to the rush and strain of modern living. For the cacti, generally, are not at all culturally exacting which is very natural since through the centuries they have been conditioned to desert aridity and to extremes of heat and cold. Therefore, if you want interesting plant forms of particularly good silhouette value which won't be even as temperamental as you are about an apartment that is torrid by day and frigid by night, which prefer neglect to watchfulness and which almost never require repotting — these are the plants for you.

A good cactus schedule runs about like this: in February and March and on into summer the plants thrive in a warm sunny window where waterings about twice a week, and an occasional brushing of the tops to remove dust, constitute the best of care; in May the cacti are sunk in their pots in some fully sunny garden bed where they can pretend through the heat that they are back home again in the desert; by September the sun will have lulled them off to sleep so that by mid-September, when they are brought in (for they are not conditioned to below freezing) all they will desire is peace and quiet to finish their rest; at this point they can be grown quite cold and so watered about twice a month or; if you want them immediately in the window garden, quite warm and so watered once a week. (If no outdoor garden is available, keep them in summer at a sunny window which is often open or plunge them in a porch or window box full of sand.)

If repotting is necessary — and you are likely to have plants for two or three years before it is — January is the time, just as the cacti are finishing their rest and preparing to grow green and plump again and maybe, though you are not to count on it, bloom. Pots for cacti are kept just as small as possible, really hardly larger than the base measurement of the plants themselves, and the earth is well firmed about their meager roots. When adding more soil, be generous with sand since a gritty mixture containing a little lime is ideal. And allocate a full quarter of the pot to a drainage layer of broken brick or broken flower pot. Water thoroughly once after potting to settle the new base and then let the plants go again on the dry side except that as new growth develops somewhat more moisture will be used up.

Cacti are easy to grow from seed or from small pieces of green new growth taken in April or May. These are cut off and allowed to dry before they are inserted about one-half inch deep in small pots of sandy soil.

Up to this point, we trust that we have successfully concealed the fact that we are not desert cactus enthusiasts. The fact is we like to fuss with plants and we prefer those of a less somnolent and turgid nature which enjoy our frequent ministrations. We like especially quick actors like our Pellionia vine which by actual measurement has grown four inches in a day. This behavior makes us feel a good time has been had by all and an enthusiastic boarder has applauded our best efforts. Also we like plants that are more reliable about flowering. However, we have neither a Mexican game room nor a modern apartment for cacti and anyway our aversion is purely personal.

If desert cacti are right for your house and your schedule, why, go ahead — enjoy them.

10. Seven Colorful Calla Lilies

DRAMATIC in leaf, bud and blossom, the calla lily with its bold outline, firm texture and tendency to repeated flowering, is the ally of every woman eager for a winter garden featuring flowers. Even one bulb introduces effective color there, while several steal the show completely during the long dominance of their bloom.

And callas are easy enough to grow. Although theirs is an elegant, aristocratic beauty, no tiresome struggle lies behind the finished product. Plenty of sunshine and water and 55 to 60° F. temperature cover the needs of strong healthy stock, which may be of dwarf or giant type bearing flowers white, yellow, pink or "black."

The old-fashioned treasured white is *Zantedeschia* (or *Richardia*) *aethiopica*. Two to three feet tall, it develops so fast that bulbs potted in August may unfurl their first enchanting spathes before Christmas. A three-months span is a good allowance, although it has been possible to get this flowering business down to a month by using warm water. This haste makes waste, since after such a speed-up, the plants will not bloom again the same season, whereas under a less impatient system every aethiopica bulb may be counted on for four or five flowers, each charmingly fresh and perfect for ten to fourteen days.

Numerous varieties of aethiopica have the parents' strength and merit of repeated bloom but they are not so tall, an asset for most window gardens where the arrangement of plants at different levels is often as important as their individual beauty. Aethiopica from this point of view is not gregarious so we usually enjoy our plants in individual settings, placing each one in an ornamental pot on a deep window sill where the handsome arrow-shaped leaves are strongly silhouetted against the light.

Of aethiopica's relatives, the Godfrey Everblooming is notably floriferous but the flowers are smaller and the plants not quite so tall. The real miniature or Baby Calla with ten or twelve blooms a season grows but twelve to eighteen inches high and is especially nice with red poinsettias.

Dormancy for all of these whites, which have been at work since the previous August, is encouraged by

June first even though lusty growth seems to deny the need. Bulbs keep stronger, however, and a better show can be forecast for the next season, if at this time water is gradually withheld and the pots laid on their sides for the summer, either outdoors along a fence or house wall or indoors in a cool cellar.

The golden calla, Z. *elliottiana*, is magnificent when grouped in the corners of a sunroom where below 60° F. temperatures will not be at all harmful. A giant of the family, this calla produces golden five-inch flowers and silver-spotted leaves. The round, flat corms are not planted until November when they are placed in six-inch pots with a one-inch covering of soil. Flowers appear around Easter time but only one, rarely two, to a plant. For this type a four-months planting-to-blooming period is usual. Dormancy is induced early in July.

A calla infrequently seen, although generally offered by seedsmen, is rehmanni, a twelve-to-fifteen-inch native of Natal with a pretty succession of lasting pink to deep rose blooms. The only house plant we have ever grown which retained its freshness as long as the pink calla was the anthurium or flamingo flower. Although rehmanni cannot equal its ten weeks' record, it does keep fresh for three weeks and may be counted upon for an all winter display.

In the rare class is the black and yellow calla, melanoleuca, now growing on our window sill. It was such a stony looking bit when we planted it that, as usual when dealing with melanoleuca, we had a nothing-will-ever-come-of-this feeling, but in just twenty-three days, green points appeared and grew until the plant reached twenty inches. Rehmanni is likewise a puzzler as to which side is up. No harm seems to result, however, from an upside-down start so long as the tubers are carefully righted when the error is apparent.

Solomon's lily, the "black" calla, really an arum, is of the same height as melanoleuca with dull, black-green spathes, maroon-tinged within. This "black" calla is slow to germinate but other varieties grow readily enough from seed sown in spring or summer.

Calla tubers may be planted at practically any time but early autumn potting makes possible the realization of their finest qualities as indoor flowering subjects. A good plan is to provide six-inch pots for aethiopica and elliottiana and four-inch containers for the dwarf miniatures and for rehmanni and melanoleuca. Half an inch of soil is spread over the tubers and ample allowed at the top of the pot to receive water. Two-thirds stiff loam and one-third leafmold or humus makes a good mixture. To prevent rot, manure and chemical fertilizers are omitted and bone flour worked into the soil instead, a tablespoon to each pot. At the three or four leaf stage, a light surface dusting of bone flour is also applied and repeated every three weeks until the period of rest.

New plantings are well moistened and then placed in a cool spot, 55 to 60° F., while they occupy themselves about rooting. During this time of dim light watering is slight and often can be omitted entirely. When in three or four weeks top growth appears, the plants are exposed to light and a warmer temperature preferably under 70° F., however. Too high heat results in lush, spindly growth and discoloration of leaf edges. When the flower stalk develops plants are moved to the sun.

The mature callas require a great deal of moisture so that two waterings a day are usually necessary after leaf development commences. To avoid any drying out, gardeners often slip the original pot into a container one or two sizes larger and wedge the space between with spagnum moss which can readily be kept moist, or else the plants are placed in deep saucers containing an inch of water.

After the summer's rest, the tubers are lifted, cleaned, relieved of any soft spots with a sharp knife and dusted with sulphur. Then they are repotted in fresh soil, and so go on year after year, sometimes for half a century with their pleasing pageant of white, yellow, rose or "black" winter blooms.

11. The Spectacular Cyclamen

LOVELY, perhaps the loveliest of all long-flowering, winter-bright plants, the Persian cyclamen is as satisfactory as an old-fashioned investment, rich in dividends. Often we select it as our plant of the year and use it as the dominant theme of the window garden. There three rose, cerise or red-brushed white plants suffice to make it a cyclamen picture as one blossom after another is poised amidst the enduring green of fern and vine.

We prize the cyclamen too as the finest of all occasional plants often relying on it for a special welcome to friends in the quiet gray, green and yellow of the guest room. There in each deep window we place a soft pink variety. Frequently in this way a warm-hued plant serves the decorative purpose of accent for a cool-hued room.

And a well-nurtured cyclamen can be counted on to keep its handsome looks for a full three months of effective bloom, if first a *healthy*, well-grown specimen with three or four blooms and thirty or more large and small buds has been selected and second — and this is absolutely essential — it is grown most of the time very cool and quite wet. If you have ever carefully picked out the most lovely cyclamen a greenhouse afforded for a gift and then a day later seen it, after the unknowing recipient had placed it in a warm room and let it dry out a little overnight, you know that no other plant that grows can, in so short a time, match the completeness of its demise.

The florist cultivates the cyclamen at 50° F., but in our houses it will stand 60° F., little more with safety. Shivery temperatures are therefore ideal for this plant which in any year will thrive in a barely heated sunroom, perfecting there its last tiny bead of a bud and retaining its beauteous gray-green foliage to the end.

At least two hours of morning sunshine are essential and the same constant supply of water beneath the plant as delights the African violet, that is, about a regularly maintained inch. Moisture is kept from the crown and the leaves cleaned by dusting with a camel's hair paint brush. If any discoloration occurs, the damaged leaves are sharply cut off, the water removed from the saucer for half a day and a fumigating layer of camphor flakes spread there to arrest the activities of the mite which may be at work. Often such treatment must be repeated in a few days. More likely *dryness of soil or air or too much warmth*, which destroy with hurricane speed, is the cause of sickliness.

Sometimes, however, florists tell us that considerable mite infection, which has previously been kept under control by greenhouse conditions, may be the cause of yellowing foliage in the home. If, therefore, your new plant, *grown cool and wet*, develops during *its first week* with you an alarming number of yellow leaves, it may not be your fault. Don't blame the florist though until you have carefully checked your own cultural practices!

When, toward April, active growth wanes and leaves naturally deteriorate, water is gradually withheld until in a few weeks the top of the plant is quite dry and easily removed. Then the exposed corm, resting properly a little above the soil surface, is dusted with powdered sulphur and the pot is placed on its side in a dark cool room, and there lightly watered about once in two weeks. In mid-May it is taken outside and laid on its side by a house wall. Here it is occasionally watered.

When new sprouts appear in August the cyclamen is repotted in a container one size larger, in rich, light garden soil mixed with a little tobacco dust as further mite protection. Care is taken in repotting not to loosen all the soil about the corm and to set this in the pot again so that it protrudes about half an inch above the soil surface. The top is then actually on a line with the pot rim.

Until early September the now actively growing cyclamen remains under an arbor or on the shaded porch. Then, well before frost, it is brought back to its cool east window.

Future results are now problematical. Some enthusiasts get new cyclamens regularly from the florist feeling "they are not worth holding over." Others find that in subsequent years bloom is freer but the individual flowers are smaller. A friend on a Kansas farm, however, has six-year-old cyclamens in seven-inch pots which bloom yearly with thirty blossoms at one time. She swears by plenty of rotted cow manure in the soil, summering on the shaded porch and a unique system of watering. She replaces the standing water daily by pouring *boiling* water into the bowls in which the plants are supported on wooden blocks. The blocks provide a steady moisture sponge while the hot water affords a fine humidifying mist.

It is our plan in fall, from the time of the appearance of the first bud, until the perfecting of the last, to give extra food each fortnight. This strengthens the cyclamen during these hard-working months. Weak liquid manure, about three tablespoons for a large well-moistened plant, is carefully spooned around the rim of the pot, or plant food tablets are inserted into the soil according to the manufacturer's directions.

Instead of being held over, cyclamens can also be kept coming in fine, generous new crops by the yearly sowing of seed which develops beautiful true-from-name varieties. It takes patience though since the process at shortest is a twelve-months business and more likely to be fifteen.

Yearly purchase of cyclamens may seem an extravagance. It depends whether time or money is the more valuable commodity in your life. Growing cyclamens from seed is a fascinating horticultural experience. Holding over the corms and repotting is also often worth the trouble. If it's the picture that pleases you, rather than the growing, however, and if your thumb has had little green experience, our counsel is—buy!

12. Ferns Require Wisdom

TIME was when the *pièce de résistance* of every parlor was a fern. Although no longer considered indispensable to interior decoration, a fern in the right place is still a really nice house plant, its soft green foliage as tranquil indoors as a dappled glen of maidenhair outside on an August day.

The lovely Maidenhair, however, is *not* the fern for the window garden. It is perhaps the most difficult one to grow indoors and not to be attempted, even as an indulgence, unless several other kinds of ferns have proved that they like your home. If you insist on trying the Maidenhair, the soil must be humusy with a touch of sharp sand. It will exist only in a cool, moist atmosphere and with no more sunlight than an east window affords. Add to this plenty of water, but never standing water.

The Boston fern, two decades ago, was a belle among house plants. Modern, more compact homes have little room to spare for a full-sized healthy specimen, and certainly should have no room whatsoever for the sickly looking, yellow, nibbled-at-the-edges plant into which this buxom beauty can deteriorate when rooms are hot, dry and dusty and sunlight relentless.

If you have the space and decorative scheme into which a Boston fern will fit, certainly there is no reason for denying yourself one of the innumerable variations which have been bred from the clean-cut parent Sword fern (*Nephrolepis*). One of our neighbors has a fascinating Boston type which reveals its ancestry in seven different kinds of leaves flourishing in wholesale abundance on the one plant. Thus some fronds are fuzzy masses of green, others are plumed and curled or fine cut into as many variations as a lady's coiffure. Whitmani with plume-like, light green leafage and the more upright, curled Verona are both interesting possibilities.

Better choices, especially for the apartment dweller, are Rabbitsfoot fern or the Holly. Rabbitsfoot takes its name from the furry rhizomes at the base of the plant which often creep out to the rim of the pot. The graceful, lacy fronds are an acceptable substitute for Maidenhair. The holly fern is a sturdier character with glossy, tough brilliant green fronds subdivided into sections reminiscent in outline of a holly leaf.

Both ferns will stand a warm room with a fairly dry atmosphere and a rabbitsfoot will even take up happy residence in a window garden with an east or west exposure. The leather fern with simple, clean cut fronds similar to these of the Boston fern's chief ancestor is equally thrifty.

In fact, these three can usually be counted permanent residents. With understanding care, in a few short years they will graduate from the three-inch pots in which they came from the florist's to six-inch ones. Not in a single leap, however.

We have seen the Birdsnest fern kept successfully for many months in the lounge at a country club but it has not always responded to our tender ministrations at home. The simple leaves, shiny, light green, and uncut with an undulating edge, grow from the crown of the plant in such a way as to make the name seem eminently appropriate.

The small Pteris ferns are usually sold indiscriminately under the label of table ferns. They are tempting in their grace, comparatively diminutive in size and variation. Fronds are often deeply cut or lobed or marked with white. They have a fragility, though, which usually grants them a brief existence in our warm living rooms. *Pteris cretica* is one of the safest.

Coming as they do in small pots, several chosen for interesting outline and markings might be grouped in a basket or on a tray. So arranged, they can be easily transported to the window for light or to the sink for a daily shower, supplying that moisture without which they shrivel. Then for company purposes the container of plants can be moved temporarily to that decorative spot which would be so culturally impossible for twenty-four hours days on end.

Ferns are only pleasing when they are growing vigorously. Any one of several factors will check normal growth. The atmosphere usually is too dry, making artificial humidity a must. But if that has been taken care of, a temperature range of 55 to 65° F. is ideal for most ferns. Too much sunlight, a misunderstood soil mixture, poor drainage, overwatering, white fly, scale — any of these are also enough to start a fern on the downward path of ill-health and ugliness.

The healthy fern grows rapidly and will need to be repotted annually every spring, the earlier the better. Winter marks the end of its resting period so fresh soil and room to grow are encouraged by repotting. The best soil mixture contains both peatmoss and leafmold to contribute porosity and facilitate drainage. Everyone who grows a fern has her special recipe. You might try three parts garden soil mixed with one part peatmoss, one part leafmold, one of sand plus a bit of crumbled charcoal.

Ample provisions must be made for drainage. A layer of broken crock rather than a single piece over the hole in the bottom of the pot, then an inch or more of rough material or pebbles over which is spread a thin layer of sphagnum moss, is drainage insurance under the loose soil mixture. Daily watering is the rule for ferns but so gauged that soil will be fairly dry on the morrow.

Soggy moisture at the roots must be avoided at all costs. The fern is one type of house plant which reacts better to watering from the top. Hence as much as you may like the jardiniere from Aunt Minnie, smash it rather than let it insidiously hold from day to day any excess water which has come through the well-drained soil in the fern pot. In the interests of shiny cleanliness a weekly sponging or spraying of the fern depending on the type of frond, is inescapable.

During late winter, when sun is not strong anyway and ferns are coming out of their resting stage, they can stand the full sunlight from an east or west window. The rest of the year, the good light is sufficient. The shadiest spot in the garden, the porch or the north window, are preferred summer vacation spots.

Health is also promoted by cutting off broken fronds at any time of the year especially in the fall when like trees, ferns are starting to rest. The slender green runners which appear in midwinter at the base of the plant are snipped off unless new ferns are desired.

Again we repeat, only a healthy fern is attractive. And so many things must be controlled to keep a fern healthy that the window gardener's ingenuity is tested to the full. Moist atmosphere and a relentless watch for scale and white fly are the cornerstones on which success rests, after correct planting and a suitable location have been arranged.

13. Emphatic Foliage for Accent

GRANDMOTHER'S house was not complete without its

palm and not so many years ago, you undoubtedly had a snake plant in your hall. Between these two cycles occurred the heyday of the aspidistra, the golden age of the rubber plant and the boom market in Boston ferns. The possibilities of greenery, however, are not confined to such fads. Plants of real beauty and distinctive silhouette will be found today in local shops. It is more than likely that such luxuriant greenness will be heightened by splashes of bronze, stripes of cream and flecks of white, rose or gold. A foliage plant, like a set of dishes, should be chosen because you like it, and not because Mrs. Smith across the street is featuring it. These plants are a long-term investment, less fussy than any in the window garden and tough enough to survive with a minimum of care.

Selected with discrimination the larger foliage plants add that final decorative touch to many modern rooms. Dracaenas, especially those marked with color, might attractively fill in a deep window sill facing east. The elegant aralia deserves a handsome container and a position within the room where its symmetry and foliage will show advantageously. With a little imagination and good taste, any one of these plants becomes the warm accent for many a room otherwise forlorn.

The fiddle-leaved rubber plant has an air of distinction that far surpasses the old-fashioned droopy type. The chief beauty of these fairly tall plants are large shining leaves, violin-shaped. The only trick involved in keeping it ornamental is sponging off the leaves once a week. Watering won't be necessary more than twice a week.

Here indeed is the perfect tall plant with clean straight lines for the light empty corner of the library or sun-room.

The Dracaena or corn plant may in time grow as tall as the rubber plant. But that will be years after you have filled your window sill with them. Taller plants do bear a striking resemblance to the waving field corn and so, as one might imagine, are a good focal point in a large room where perspective and silhouette can be featured. They prefer a temperature of 60 to 70° F. and a soil that has not been rammed down too hard in the pot. Again the weekly sponging of the foliage is necessary for full beauty and, in this case, to prevent red spider.

Breadth rather than height is furnished by Pandanus or screw pine. It seldom grows more than three feet tall but will need fully that much width so that a careless brushing by passersby does not injure its perfect symmetry. The long swordlike leaves which spring from a center crown are green and white, edged with sharp spines.

The pandanus does not thrive on neglect. A sunny window where the temperature is seldom less than 65° F. is comfortable. From October to January water is given twice a week and then from the base of the pot to prevent decay from moisture seeping into the crown of the plant. Foliage is cleansed by wiping in the direction of the sharp spines with a soft, damp cloth. In January, when active growth begins, daily watering is necessary. That is also the month for repotting, if necessary, and in February new plants may be started from the suckers which have appeared.

Aspidistra and snake plant are suitable in height for bookcases and tables. Nothing except freezing has been known to kill either one. The aspidistra's nickname of saloon plant is testimony of its tenacious hold on life. Though you may be weary of both of these plants, they're worth keeping around for the leaves which may be cut for flower arrangements. Either the broad green slender stemmed leaves of aspidistra or the spiky and mottled lengths of sansevieria are a serviceable background for a few accent flowers, such as three carnations, or a camellia during winter. Their care involves nothing more than moderate watering and regular cleansing of the foliage. Neither one demands a summer in the garden but will remain satisfied to be a house plant twelve months of the year.

Dieffenbachias are neither more nor less distinguished than any fairly large-leaved green plant. They are slow growing so their eighteen-inch to two-foot height does not too quickly outdistance the place for which they were chosen. Warmth, moisture, light but not bright sunshine, and clean foliage keep them happy.

Most symmetrical of all foliage plants is the evergreen Araucaria or Norfolk Island Pine. The needle-like foliage lends itself to decoration at Christmas time and it is enchanting as a table tree. The branches appear at regular intervals along the center stem and each set at the same level forming another circle of green indicates a year's growth. New leaves are a signal for a meal of fertilizer.

Araucaria will need repotting only when its container is crammed with roots. It grows well in any loamy soil such as that of a rose bed or pasture land. Judicious watering is the key to long term cultivation. Water must reach all of the roots but should never be allowed to stand in the saucer. Apply a lot rather than a little at a time whenever the soil is moderately dry. An occasional syringing will keep the plant free from dust and insects.

Aralia is almost feathery with its fragile palm-like leaves borne in profusion. It has an inherent grace which is heightened when a specimen flecked with gold or white is found.

The A B C's of keeping these foliage plants as handsome at home as in the greenhouse revolve around light and watering. No one of them should be overwatered; two or three times a week will be sufficient. Nor is repotting necessary every year. The amount of roots in the pot settles whether it will be every second year or every three. The final boon is the fact that they are satisfied with light, although the sun in an east or west window will do no harm. Find the foliage plant you like, care for it intelligently and keep an easy mind on the score that it need not be smothered with attention.

14. Engaging Green Things

NEITHER breath-taking nor essential but far more durable than their flower-bedecked window mates are the smaller

green things which grow less than a foot high. Every
fall it seems as though the florist has new ones of this
kind for us to try. Upon his assurance that they are
either naturally dwarf or slow growing, we triumphantly
bear homeward our newest acquisitions.

These small plants, which depend on their foliage and
their manner of growing to entice us, are invaluable to
fill in blank spots in the window garden and to round
out the setting of restful green. Then too, since they
are foliage plants, which can live comfortably on light
or diluted sunlight, they are suitable for use on a coffee
table or mantelpiece, indeed on any spot in a room
which would be enhanced by "some green thing growing".

No plant better illustrates the principle of tucking-in
than *Helxine soleiroli*, lowest growing of all. You may
know it as Baby's Tears, Pollyanna, Mother of Thousands,
Irish moss, or Corsican carpet plant. Whatever nickname it is given, helxine is impossible to kill, unless
you forget to water it for weeks at a time, and it is the
easiest plant in the world to start off again in a new pot.
A section smaller than a fifty-cent piece can be taken
from a thriving plant, pressed into the soil of a three-
inch pot and kept watered. It may look dead for a time
but presto — it will soon be busily clambering over the
edge of its container.

For a row of three- to six-inch plants on the mantelpiece, or the east or west window sill, or in a harmoni-
ously colored pot on the coffee table, Peperomia or
Maranta are good choices. Peperomia with its thick

shiny leaves takes the dry heat of apartments in its stride. It, too, is easily propagated by cuttings. These chubby plants actually like warmth and they also like humidity, so the pebble-filled tray again comes into use. The variegated leaved, stemless *Peperomia sandersi* is easiest to find but the taller glossy green ones are nothing at which to turn up one's nose.

Maranta with its distinctively marked and variegated foliage is a pleasing contrast. The spots or bars may be yellow or brown, red or white. It is interesting to observe the habits of the leaves. New ones unfurl delicately and flat open ones, like good children rising for their elders, reach up vertically every evening so as to face each other. Perhaps you've heard it called, because of this, Prayer Plant.

As distinguished and tropical in origin as maranta is Syngonium, which unfortunately has no common name. The arrow-shaped leaves, often deeply cut, are held aloft on slender swaying stems. There may be great variations in the size and lobing of leaves and in the variegation. This is slow growing rather than low growing, and after many years may develop into a climbing plant. It delights in heat, humidity and plenty of moisture.

A few years ago, the Pick-a-Back plant, Tolmiea, took indoor gardeners by storm. Sooner or later during winter tiny new clusters of leaves appear at the base of many old ones. Of course, the entire leaf is removed and, inserted in a pot of sandy soil, will root and become an individual plant. Nothing is more luxuriant appearing than the thrifty pick-a-back. Unless this plant is kept fairly cool and in an east or west window, mealy bug is sure to take up its abode. One winter ours met with a casualty of different sort, for our dog decided pick-a-back was an excellent substitute for grass. The poor plant spent most of the winter chewed back to a few scrubby stems!

Sometimes our florist has an assortment of small house plants which are better known as green garden shrubs in warmer climates. But all of them have in three years time proved dependable additions to the east window garden. Pittosporum is well shaped like a small tree with a rounded head. Around the main stem small woody ones cluster in a whorl, and the tufts of dark green ovate leaves are renewed every spring.

Osmanthus or holly olive, which adds about two inches to its stature every year, has good silhouette value. The small leaves are holly leaves in miniature, complete to the sharp tips. The side branches from a center stem gradually make a vertical growth which make it an accent plant for the window comparable to Lombardy poplar outdoors.

Any one of these small foliage plants might flower. Therein lies neither their chief beauty nor value. The flowers are for the most part odd and inconspicuous and usually so infrequent as to be one of those "once in a lifetime" affairs. We select these engaging green things for their greenness, their thriftiness, their form and their size.

They have no whims. We keep them growing by giving them light or the limited sunlight of an east or west window. The weekly shower bath not only keeps them fresh but wards off incipient red spider or mealy bug. They will thrive on humidity but adjust themselves to heat plus moisture.

A resting period is in most cases not noticeable. Perhaps a decline in vigor will be apparent during summer and fall but for the most part plants remain static without losing any of their display charm. They may, it is true, be rested during summer in the shadiest part of the house plants' vacation land but they will also hold the window fort in a modest way while tired beauties are recuperating. Their cool greenness is refreshing indoors on a hot day.

15. Fruiting Plants Are Fun, Too

FRUITING plants with their bright burdens of scarlet, orange and yellow have many charming possibilities for a house which can provide them really cool accommodation. At Christmas time we often adorn our tier table with an Otaheite orange tree on the top and a group of Cleveland or Christmas cherries below with a mass of self-branching Pittsburgh ivy to set them off. An old-fashioned wooden step plant stand painted red and placed with various fruit plants and green vines in the cool sunroom has also given us a lot of pleasure at various times.

There are nice possibilities among these fruiting shrubs. Not every florist carries each kind every year although a few are always available. The Otaheite orange, the Ponderosa lemon and that jewel of a small tree, the coral ardisia, *Ardisia crenulata*, incline to be rather expensive but the cherry, the pepper plant and the pomegranate, *Punica granatum nana*, never run very high and all do keep attractive for some months provided they can be placed in about a 60° F. temperature. If this is impossible, by no means invest, for it is simply sickening to have the experience, which so many enthusiasts have had, of bringing home one of these gems for prominent placement only to watch it shed its fruit and leaves and die before your very eyes within some forty-eight hours.

Next to cool living is the matter of deep watering. These are all rather shrubby subjects so beware relying entirely on the little-and-often top moistening system. Rather supplement this by setting each plant once weekly in a pail of water filled to within an inch of the pot rim and let it remain until the top soil feels moist. Then remove it.

Spray the tops occasionally too, perhaps while the plant is taking its deep drink and has been removed from its more tidy location. And if any of these plants are ornamentally set in a jardiniere, slip a block of wood or an inverted saucer beneath them to hold them above any possible standing residue of water. This always leads to trouble.

The Orange and Lemon trees from the florist hold their fruit through the late autumn and early winter. In March tops are lightly trimmed and the worn-out top soil replaced by a fresh mixture. Soon a little cloud of fragrant blossoms appears and through the summer develops into fruit. Once this is perfected, the plants enter a relative state of rest and are therefore grown from October to February as near 50° F. as is consistent with their decorative use. During this period they harden their wood and prepare for next year's bloom. They will need less water now but must not go entirely dry or the evergreen foliage will fall, especially if temperatures are a bit higher than they like. They will stand up to 65° F., of course, and like plenty of sun even when at rest.

When these citrus fruits are raised from home-saved seed or from cuttings, fruiting rarely occurs. It takes aeons of time for seedlings to fruit and, furthermore, it is usually a matter of budding or grafting too. So save and plant the seed from the breakfast oranges if you wish but for your pains expect only nice little evergreen plants.

The coral Ardisia is one of the most fascinating Christmas plants of all. Not only are its colors traditional when the luscious scarlet fruits hang in great bunches amidst the shining leaves but shortly afterwards the plant develops a three-tiered effect which is a special delight. At the base remain the fruits, even until June, then there is a center section cloudy with small white blooms, while at the same time new growth stretches out above. When this appears, it is time for the fortnightly dose of liquid manure to commence. The other fruiting plants also revel in this extra nutrition at any time that their new growth is developing. Scale is to be watched for and treated before your earliest convenience.

The Christmas Cherry (now the Cleveland rather than Jerusalem type), if considerately treated, is good for a long and merry life. In a cool spot it will not insultingly drop its fruit but part with it reluctantly and not till the end of February or early March. (Fruit may be dried and seed extracted for a future crop.) Leaves will fall then too. The plant is tired and desires rest.

At this point stern pruning is in order. Each branch is cut back to two eyes or buds—you can feel these little swellings along the wood—and the plant is moved to an even colder but still frost-free spot. About 40° F. is good, and in full light. Little water will now be needed, not oftener then twice a month anyway.

When in late spring top growth reappears, the cherry is brought again to its 50 to 60° F. spot to wait removal to the outdoors in May. From the first of July on to its fruiting time, which away from the greenhouse may not occur until February, the plant is given the fortnightly feeding. No touch of frost must reach it outside and inside it must be free of even the slightest taint of illuminating or coal gas to which it is highly allergic.

In the summer these fruiting plants, repotted only if necessary, but with top soil replaced by a fresh mixture are plunged in semi-shade or else set on the porch. All through the outdoor months plenty of water and extra food is important since they are not resting like the geranium and cyclamen but working hard to prepare their bright fruits for your next winter's pleasure.

16. The Gardenia Is Never Easy

GARDENIAS are flowering plants which are either cursed or adored. People never have just medium feelings about them. If with careful nurture they achieve a state of health which produces a long and lovely fragrant waxen succession of bloom, then the hosannas rise but if after infinite pains, those numerous fat buds one day come cannonading down with horrible finality, then even a lady's vocabulary is strained. Now what are the rules for gardenias?

Probably the best rule is to leave this plant where it really belongs — in a greenhouse. There temperature, ventilation and humidity can all be regulated to the exacting tastes of this temperamental Southern belle. Still even though exasperating, the gardenia has often enough responded to painstaking gardeners dealing with ordinary house conditions to make it obvious that this plant can be a house plant.

The gardenia proves most amenable to home discipline when grown at 60° F. in the daytime, with a drop no lower than to 55° F. at night. These are the temperatures favored by florists. It proves fairly tolerant, however, of heat up to 70° F. but when grown so warm, the plant is more susceptible to attacks of mealy bug. (If these appear, or red spider, treatment must be prompt and eradication immediate.)

The gardenia wants a place in the morning sun and is benefited when the foliage is syringed with water at least once a week, but still better once a day. This wetting of leaves helps to compensate for a dry house atmosphere which can be further alleviated by the pebble tray or saucer device. When tops have been sprayed, however, the plant is kept out of the sun until they have dried.

Since this plant is a shrub with fairly heavy roots, frequent top watering is not always adequate. To insure saturation of the lowest roots, it is a good plan about once a week to let the plant get just dry enough for the top soil to lose its otherwise barely moist feeling. Then the gardenia is set in a pail filled with water to within an inch of the pot rim. There it remains until the earth on the surface feels damp, a sign that sufficient moisture has been absorbed through the pot walls to reach the entire root system. This for a very large plant might be a matter of hours. Meanwhile tops might also be well syringed above and below and the whole plant thus reconditioned for another week's battle against unfriendly elements.

Extra nutrients are best supplied in the form of plant tablets or liquid manure. Neither is necessary for the first month after the gardenia comes from the florist. Thereafter monthly applications appear to be most satisfactory unless in summer the plant seems to reach a standstill. Then stimulation is checked and the plant permitted to enjoy a natural rest. When new leaves indicate active growth has commenced again, the feeding schedule is resumed.

Baffled enthusiasts often feel certain that all the gardenia needs to regain its health is repotting in a larger container. Yet rarely does this prove to be the hoped-for panacea since the gardenia grows slowly at best and the florist's plant is usually adequately supplied with root room for one year anyway and often two.

When toward the end of the second spring, it does begin to outgrow its quarters (if by a miracle it has survived that long) it is provided with a pot one size larger. Into this it is transferred carefully, its shrubby roots intact and the tight earth ball unbroken. Extra soil, full of humus, is packed around it while an inch layer of drainage material is most carefully fitted over the drainage hole in the bottom of the pot. Late May is the best time for this major operation because immediately afterwards the well syringed plant can recover from post-operative shock under the pleasant humid conditions of the open porch or the lightly shaded and sheltered garden bed into which it can be plunged. Here frequent syringing and watering must be attended to during any periods of dry summer weather.

Through the outdoor months some buds may form. It is best to nip these promptly in order to conserve the gardenia's energy for winter flowering. Sometimes too in summer a bit of pruning needs doing if one branch grows too far beyond the others and so destroys the pleasing symmetry of an otherwise shapely plant. By the end of August or the first week in September, the gardenia is returned to its eastern window where the shade is drawn if the sun gets overly hot during end-of-the-season days.

We are often asked if new gardenias can't be started from the old ones, or even from a corsage bloom carefully kept fresh in a glass of water. Sometimes, yes, these end pieces of young growth will root, but really the propagation of gardenias requires not only the expert's hand but also his greenhouse.

17. Geraniums for Gaiety

SCARLET geraniums preening themselves in the sun are the gayest plants in the world. That's why we consider them the perfect alleviation for our dull eastern winters and so often go in for them in a big way, some years giving them exclusive possession of our very best and sunniest window.

Once geraniums were considered the least temperamental of house plants. Actually this is not so. They have a variety of idiosyncrasies to be considered if lavish and long bloom — that is from October through March — is your desire. First there must be a flood of sunshine, all the hours your brightest south or east window can afford. Even there through a succession of dull winter weeks budding will be sparse. You must then be patient, realizing it is the factor of sunlight which is lacking and not start a wild repotting or fertilizing program.

Next, geraniums require both a cool location, even down to 45° F. and certainly not above 65° F., a certain amount of humidity (we favor the pebble tray over frequent top syringing which is not only a terrific chore for a windowful of plants but, unless evaporation is rapid, sometimes leads to leaf and stem decay), tight potting in a rather heavy soil and water only after they dry out. A thorough soaking is then in order. Plants must also be turned frequently at the window and fed liquid manure every other week.

When in winter once stocky young plants grow lank with lush soft growth, unduly small and yellow leaves appear, and blooms are imperfect as well as infrequent, it is time to check over these essential health factors — sun, coolness, humidity, pot size and frequency of watering. Are you perhaps killing them with kindness by watering every day or have you coddled them to the extent of excluding all fresh air?

When your day to day culture is right, there is still another big determining factor which influences bloom — condition of rest. Geraniums are good for a mighty show six months or a bit more at a stretch. But they are incapable of a twelve-month production scheme. Too often gardeners surveying in September a bed or porch full of flowering geraniums have the idea that bringing these indoors is all that is necessary to insure a continuous winter pageant.

Such plants, however, are at that time on the weary side. They are summer-spent and, unless already in pots, of no further flowering use until next May. Potted specimens, however, may have early value for the house if they still show signs of more buds and are shapely and full of leaf growth. Toward the end of September give these some liquid manure, stir up the top soil with a fork and bring them to a sunny window in a room where many hours of fresh air are possible for the first two weeks.

When finally, after about a month, no new buds open, cut the plants back to approximately three pieces of three-inch growth. Set them away in a cool light place (50° F. is fine) and water once a week or less until about January when growth becomes more determinedly active. Then bring them again to the sun, water freely and apply the liquid fertilizer. By the end of February buds will appear again, perhaps earlier.

Such is essentially a salvage campaign which provides some indoor geranium bloom in early and late winter. For steadier effect, grow your own plants from cuttings made in late May or June from any older plants you have or else order them before July from the florist. Otherwise he won't have them, for it seems that both public and purveyor are again creatures of habit. Although many a window garden would be grand with young geraniums in October, it hasn't been the custom to demand them then. Hence this showiest of indoor flowering plants simply cannot be obtained before late winter unless ordered ahead.

If you do order, these are glorious kinds—the bright red Olympic or Improved Ricard, the exceedingly choice salmon-pink Beaute Poitevine, or Picardy, the rose pink Enchantress Fiat and the pure white Madame Recamier. Consider the room and your accessories. We like reds as companions for our copper lustre ware, the salmon pink with our precious lavender glass oddments and the white Recamier to go with poinsettias in a Christmas picture. One kind a season is the best, we find, for a strong pictorial effect.

Now if you handle the whole matter yourself with no dependence on a florist, take cuttings (see method page 180) from your older plants at the time of the house-to-garden transfer in late May or June.

By August, sturdy young plants will have developed which will be ready for separate potting. They will begin setting blooms in September but these first ones are pinched off to let the plant strengthen its leafy frame for a hard winter's work. At the time of the August potting in three-inch containers a firm soil mixture is supplied. We use less humus and sand and more garden loam than for most house plants. The idea is for the soil to feel quite firm and stiff.

Older geraniums are not discarded in spring if there will be suitable accommodation for their larger size next winter. With each branch relieved of five or six inches of growth and the roots shifted on to a next larger pot size or else resuscitated by the addition of some fresh soil mixture in the scooped-out upper layer of soil, they are plunged in a fairly sunny garden stretch. There these plants develop into brilliant winter specimens. Every bud must, however, be pinched off through the summer and enough turning of the pot and top trimming attended to, to produce a fine symmetrical plant.

For indoor gardening geraniums are in our opinion right up front with the wax begonias for ease of culture and brilliance of bloom. The important thing is to understand their few basic expectations and then to establish a routine growth cycle to give you fresh plants in fall when you want them.

18. The Hearty Hydrangea

HYDRANGEAS usually enter our homes with the Easter parade of gift plants. If they are then set in a light place and watered about every time you turn around, for they do seem to have an eternal thirst, they will hold fresh flowers for a long time and be in nice green condition for the outdoor transfer in May.

Then comes the momentous decision — to place them in the garden for good or prepare them for a return to house routine. In many parts of the country these forcing types of hydrangea are but doubtfully hardy so if in your garden a lot of the chrysanthemums are poor survivors, it will be best to plan to take special care of the hydrangea and mound soil over the tops from the time of the first expected hard freeze, which is usually sometime in December, until late March. An open sunny location or one shaded just a little will be fine but there must be plenty of humus in the soil and some oak leaves or acid peatmoss included if the plants are blue.

If, however, you decide that the hydrangea is dear to you as a green thing indoors and that you have space enough to enjoy it, why then here is the kind of routine it demands.

Before it embarks on vacation, cut the hydrangea back hard, shortening each stem to two sets of buds (those swellings on the stem). Then if it is in need of repotting (and it usually is) shift it on to a larger container. When it has reached tub size, do not shift unless most essential but do scrape away as much top soil as you can, and work in some fresh mixture. And if your hydrangea is a blue beauty, which you prefer to keep blue, add a tablespoon of alum to the soil mixture to acidify it or in the interests of true pinkness, substitute as much lime.

Next, plunge the potted plant in the lightly shaded garden. Set the tubbed one there on top of the ground or else give it a good light location on the porch. In either spot water your plant well and frequently and from August on, apply a cup of liquid manure twice monthly. Although the hydrangea is not now nearly so interesting as it was when you received it, it must have your regular attention since it is deeply engrossed in developing a quantity of flowering wood which will later please you.

In October a really cold but just above freezing home site must be discovered for early winter accommodations. A dim cellar or attic location with a temperature around 40° F. or a bit less will be fine. Here the plant will lose its leaves and go to sleep. If you water it once a month through this time, that will be fine.

By January the hydrangea's hibernation will be finished. Placed again in a sunny window and given plenty of water, it will wake up and get to work on its Easter dress. The liquid manure feeding schedule can now be resumed for pink plants while for blue ones an aluminum sulphate solution is better because it deepens the blue quality of the flowers. (Allow one-quarter pound to five quarts of water and apply a cup every ten days until the buds show color.)

Once the flowers have formed, their freshness is prolonged by setting the plants out of the sun. We find they look particularly attractive when placed in the empty fireplace where they definitely proclaim that at last the winter is past and "the time of the singing of birds is come."

Hydrangeas are readily propagated by cuttings. It doesn't take long and it is simple enough but it is a lot of bother and also, it must be remembered, even the first-year plants are likely to need eight-inch pots. So unless you have plenty of space for house plants as in a big sunroom, a flock of hydrangeas may be more bother than use.

This is the method: in March take off four-inch pieces of end growth (this will cut down on the parent plant's flowers for the year, of course) and insert the cut ends of these firmly three nodes deep in a big pot of half-sand, half-soil mixture which is both warm and moist; invert an old aquarium or a battery jar above the pot and keep it in the light but out of the sun.

In four or five weeks, do a little investigating. Lift one of the cuttings and if it is rooted, then transfer the lot to small separate pots of a mixture more soil than sand but still light. Place a jelly glass over each pot until the weather outside is quite warm. Then plunge the youngsters in a shady garden bed where they will need water at least once maybe twice daily. Through the summer growth will be sturdy and two shifts to larger pots necessary until finally the March cuttings are about eight-inch pot size and ready for the regular soil mixture with lime for the pinks and alum for the blues.

Their culture is now the same as for the parent plant — rest, then sun and stimulation. All this is considerable trouble which we wouldn't take because our feelings on hydrangeas are very so-so. However, if your gift plant is one of the lovely and lately introduced heavenly blues or alluring pinks we can see how you might be tempted to such a program even if we wouldn't!

19. Indoor Plants from the Outdoor Garden

THE mischievous face of a pansy, the sentimental spray of bleeding heart or a pink cloud of spiraea are as much fun in the window garden as opening that surprise package on Valentine's Day. We love the packages and we love the garden flowers that, without much coaxing, bloom so gaily at the wrong time of year.

In the fall when the window garden has just been set up, we are grateful for the color that garden flowers add to the predominant mass of green. Any of the small seedling annuals which are leading a sheltered existence under their still blooming parents are capable of an independent and highly creditable life of their own indoors. Tiny marigold or snapdragon plants, even cornflower or cosmos, may be lifted into a window box or set three in a three-inch pot of good soil to show what they can do. By late October baby blossoms of orange and red or blue and rose make a brave showing until some of the true house plants start their performance. We like to fill at least a dozen pots and mass them in fours or sixes so that a strong color effect is achieved. Or they may be transplanted, approximately four inches apart, in a long and narrow window box.

We also like to rescue before heavy frost any poky annuals that haven't yet started to flower. Stock is often a candidate and calendula and salvia are other possibilities. Once the shock of being moved to a pot is over, these all flower for an unbelievably long time indoors where their bloom is all the more appreciated because it is smaller and paler than snappy autumn weather would permit outside.

The real thrill of garden plants indoors comes in midwinter when pride in the amaryllis has lessened and the joy of bouvardia palled. Remembering this, we plan in November to relieve the boredom. A clump or two of variegated funkia is dug from the border before the ground freezes, potted and plunged in the coldframe. (If you have no coldframe, an unheated glass-enclosed sunporch will do but here we never let the plants dry out thoroughly.) Some dreary January day, we bring them into the house where warmth and regular watering persuade them that June must have come. Not being exposed to wind and weather, the leaves are especially handsome and the spikes of pale lavender blossoms a refreshing contrast to lusty cyclamen and begonias.

Violas, even violets if you have a really cold sunporch, and the trailing Vinca minor or periwinkle also will adapt themselves to this double life. The vinca can be placed in brackets at either side of the window in October. In fact, we have never forgotten how beautifully large pots of vinca framed a friend's window garden all

one winter with cascading masses of small leaved greenery studded with lavender blossoms. But if these plants
are to be ornamental, they must be sprayed vigorously
and often with cold water to ward off red spider.

The indoor gardener with a mañana complex needn't
miss out on garden plants even though nothing was
potted up in November. Some mild February day when
fingers are itching to get into the earth and soil oozes
around one's shoes, a foray can be made on the rock
garden or border to dig up clumps of bleeding heart,
astilbe or spiraea, primroses and perennial candytuft.
These are potted in a good mixture of soil and compost
or humus, soaked with water and then tucked in a cool,
dim part of the cellar until two or three inches of top
growth has been made. Then into light and liberal
watering and before it seems possible, flower buds are
peering forth shyly and rather hesitantly. It is possible
to buy clumps of spiraea for forcing or at Easter time
even flowering plants. But you'll brag more about your
own and all you suffered to dig them, yes, actually dig
them, in February.

Some say that forget-me-not and even hemerocallis
can likewise be made to flower thus unseasonably. One
autumn we intend to dig up a few of the early blooming
dwarf daylilies such as Apricot, the pale yellow Sovereign
or clear Tangerine to try for ourselves. You have probably already thought of something else in your garden that
you intend to attempt forcing.

This fairy tale is not complete without the miniature
roses. We fell for a pot of the pinky cream Pixie at a

March flower show several years ago and ever since we have bought every kind of miniature rose we could find. Tom Thumb, a semi-double crimson, Oakington Ruby, which blinks a white eye from its red flower, and Pixie have proved most satisfactory. They bloom for about two months starting in January, and no one quite believes it is really a rose in the window.

Roses also must be fooled into flowering indoors by spending a dormant period in low temperature. Therefore the plants are either purchased from a nursery or lifted from the garden and potted in November in a mixture of garden soil and peatmoss enriched with a little dried manure. They can stay in the coldframe until cold weather arrives, then be brought indoors to a sunny window where they are watered and showered regularly. They do not favor too much heat, 65° F. is the maximum for success. And when warm weather comes, out they go along the edge of the rose bed.

To mention seeds for indoor flowers now seems an anticlimax. Pansies are a possibility, if seed of winter flowering varieties is sown outdoors between May and August. The earlier they are planted, the earlier they flower in winter. Seedlings are thinned out and young plants transferred to three-inch pots, one plant for each pot. When this move has been made, they are also pinched back. Keep them on the cool side, feed with liquid manure, water and syringe regularly.

For years we have been called upon to admire Heavenly Blue morning glories which friends grew and flowered so successfully but we could not, until we discovered we were too forehanded planting seeds in October. Heavenly Blue, the red and white Cornell, ethereal Pearly Gates, or the vari-colored magnificently large-flowered Imperial hybrids, if planted in February, will flower in a sunny window in about ten weeks. Six seeds are planted in a five-inch pot and later thinned to three plants.

We were right about fall planting for clock vine or black-eyed Susan, *Thunbergia alata*. Five seeds and later three plants to a three-inch pot will flower in January and from then on endlessly. The apricot, salver-shaped blooms, often with a dark eye, add another color to the window garden.

We have been trying to entice you with fresh colors and different plants. If any added inducement is necessary, most of these provide good cut flower material for empty winter vases and when the indoor garden season is over, all of these plants return to the garden to resume a more every-day routine.

20. Kitchen to Parlor Plants

ALL plants do not come from florist or seedsman. In fact, it is amazing to consider the possibilities available in the average kitchen to any woman with an active imagination. Here from sweet potato tuber, orange seed, carrot and other material at hand, she can develop truly beautiful specimens to frame and fill any light or sunny window with pleasing verdure all winter long.

Flowers from such a source are doubtful but variety

in leaf form and color is infinite. Transferred to the parlor the loveliness of these plants will quite belie their kitchen origin and puzzle too many an enthusiast who heretofore has been certain that she knew her house plants even by their nicknames.

For framing, the sweet potato is both rapid and reliable. It grows into a pair of curtains with Jack-and-the-bean-stalk exuberance. Select an old one, not a freshly dug tuber and be certain it is plump and firm. Place this in the mouth of a mason jar or in a narrow-necked vase where it can be supported above a constant water level which covers the tip but never floats the whole potato. Either a glass or china container may be used but we like to start with glass so as to watch the forming of the first white roots and to gauge accurately in the beginning the need for extra water as evaporation takes place.

For the first ten days the sweet potato is set in a cool dark place to keep its mind on rooting. Then when the white strands are plainly visible, it is brought to the light for top growing, which we warn you is a lush undertaking. No bit of a spot will do for a sweet potato, once it is under way. Place one at each side of a big window. String wires or string up and across and you will find that twining those busy tendrils in the way they should go is as regular a morning chore as making beds.

Usually quite a number of little swellings appear and form spikes of growth. We find we get quicker and less tangled results if we pinch out all but two or three of them. This allows but one or two leafy lines for each string. To make the most of the plant decoratively, choose colorful vases or after rooting is started, carefully transfer each tuber to a deep attractive bowl filled with pebbles. There maintain a water level to touch the base just as you do with your narcissus bulbs. If it's a kitchen not a living-room window you plan to adorn, you will find a pair of bright red or yellow bowls from the cooking sets is both appropriate and attractive.

Now while we are in the root department, if you haven't thought of carrot, horseradish, and beet tops as on the decorative side, just look again at their handsome leafy tops. The ferny grace of the carrots makes them ideal for a dining-table center piece or as a spot of green for a sofa end-table or you can grow them for important placement in the window garden. The beet foliage is interesting for its red veining while the bold, arrow-shaped leaf of the horseradish is something to nurture for a silhouette position.

All three of these rapidly break into greenness if tops are cut back to within an inch of the roots and the roots themselves cut back to about one-third. These pieces are then arranged in flower bowls filled with pebbles and water which reaches them but does not submerge their tops. In a light place (table arrangements pass their days at windows) intent little green shoots soon emerge, soft and ferny or strong and hearty according to their natures.

We are told that these tops also perform nicely if inserted in three- or five-inch pots of rather sandy soil which is kept moist. This we have not tried but we can imagine how amusing it would be to have a pair of handsome horseradish plants slipped into beautiful containers and set on the deep living-room window sills. There they would undoubtedly puzzle our more horticultural friends in their search for a proper Latin name to fasten upon this friendly garden vegetable.

Orange, lemon and grapefruit trees are attractive for the shining look of their foliage. While blossom and fruit-bearing trees do not readily come out of the kitchen, exceedingly pleasant little plants do. Just wash the seeds and insert three to a five-inch pot of moist damp sand. Keep warm and shaded until sprouts appear. Then move the pots to a bright window. A little of your favorite kind of fertilizer will speed them on their shiny way once growth has been established.

Also from the South is the alligator or avocado pear which occasionally passes through our kitchens. After the pulp has been removed for a salad, the seed is supported by three toothpicks thrust into the base so that it can be suspended in a glass or jar of water where the moisture level just touches it. Here in about three weeks it is interesting to see the thick white roots push down and then the top of the strong seed burst open as Nature within insists upon the forceful principle of growth.

From the split emerges the interesting green top of a pretty little glossy-leaved avocado tree. After about two months of such growing, soil is gradually added to the water by way of transition living. Then the young plant is carefully transferred to a small pot of soil. In time it will develop in both size and beauty, spending its summers plunged in the garden, its winters as the graceful adornment of some sunroom corner.

Finally, with the children's special interests in mind we must mention the allure of the lowly kitchen lentil. Its most endearing quality is speed. Just place a layer of lentils in a saucer with enough water to moisten without floating them. Add a little more as evaporation indicates. Keep the saucer in a light window and before the week is out you will have a miniature forest of urgent lentil shoots as a decorative table center piece, or just for the sake of family fun.

21. Lilies of the Field Come In

YEARS may come and years may go but Easter lilies are always a magnet of attention during April. And if you would like some in your window garden at Easter time, there is no reason why you can't grow them. The fragrant, glistening white blooms are matchless in purity and stateliness, yet not too difficult for the most unpractised amateur.

Two or three white lilies are grown for the Easter season. *Lilium giganteum* is preferred, and of this the Croft strain, grown in the northwestern United States, is now considered the finest Easter lily available. Other pure white lilies, which double for this purpose and are suitable for forcing, are *L. Harrisi* and a Florida-grown strain of this, and *L. Creole*.

The large scaly bulbs are planted some time during October, and each one needs a tall five-inch flower pot.

A mixture of two parts good garden loam and two of leafmold or humus is a good basis for operations. A generous two-inch layer of this soil over the usual rough drainage material is firmed down in the pot and then covered with a one-inch layer of clean sand. On this the lily bulb is set and then covered with soil until only the tip shows. The pot should be little more than half filled at this stage. For the Easter lily sends up a tall and none too handsome stem which can be concealed a little as it grows and loses its lower leaves, by filling in the pot with the rich soil mixture. Thus added support is also afforded.

Immediately after planting, pots of Easter lily bulbs are set in a cool place where they receive no sunshine and only a little light. The cellar floor or a sheltered porch where they may be put underneath a bench is good. No rest period in the dark is needed. When stem and leaves have sprouted, a lighter place is required but still no direct sunlight. A temperature in the neighborhood of 60° F. is agreeable. Two months before Easter, a warmer location and sunlight for part of the day encourages flower buds. Fortnightly feeding with liquid manure is also helpful.

Time, not fussing, is the prime factor in producing home-grown Easter lilies. Heat, of approximately 60° F., with a few more degrees after the buds show, is also conducive to flower production. Lilies are probably the most glamorous and tantalizing flowers to grow outdoors. They face stiff competition in the realm of glamour from flowering plants in window gardens. Still you may wish to try others of this pedigreed family.

We have been so spoiled by the easily forced paper-white narcissus and lily-of-the-valley, that it comes as a surprise to most of us that certain species of garden lilies can be made to flower indoors. In fact, almost all of the kinds that are planted in the garden could be forced indoors with relative ease, if it were possible to obtain the bulbs during September. Since most lily bulbs are not ready for delivery until much nearer the end of the year, this is but a lovely dream and consequently forcing means little more than growing the lilies in pots for flowering earlier than in the garden.

The fragrant Regal lily is one of the trickiest. But the brilliant little coral lily, *L. tenuifolium*, the exquisite *L. speciosum* or *L. rubrum* with recurved petals flecked with red, and the vivid tiger lily, *L. tigrinum*, are relatively easy. They are potted and grown along the pattern for Easter lilies. If bulbs of these varieties can be obtained by mid-October, they are worth trying for the window garden. The flowers will be smaller and more delicately colored but they are nonetheless exquisite. as is any lily anywhere.

After flowering, the bulbs of garden varieties may be planted outdoors. Most of the Easter lily varieties are not hardy north of Washington, D. C. Since they some-times bloom again the same year in the garden and occa-sionally prove unexpectedly hardy there, you can always set your Easter lily gift-plant out — in hopes. But for any chance of success, the plant must have been watered and tended continuously and not stuck in the cellar directly the flower faded. That practice is certain death from which no garden can recall a plant.

22. The Marica, a Matchless House Plant

IF A marica can be acquired — and we say "acquired" because it covers the baser forms of attainment of which we consider the marica worthy — by all means get one. For some unknown reason growers and florists do not handle this pearl among house plants which for generations has been passed from neighbor to neighbor under the name of house iris, twelve apostles plant and toad lily.

Most descriptive is the term, house iris, since the leaves grow in an iris-like fan and the flowers, which develop near the sides on leaf-like stems are of miniature iris or orchid form and color — blue, lavender or white. Truly the house iris is a treasure in the window garden, winter-blooming, pest and disease free, tolerant of extremes of heat and cold, and only moderately demanding about sun.

But place the plant in a sunny window for most lavish results, although fair bloom may also be expected after the turn of the year in any fully light location. Be generous with water. We find our plant requiring in all seasons of active growth a thorough soaking once or twice daily and, in addition, on all not too busy mornings we hold the tops under the strong stream of the open faucet.

If the leaf tips always stay green this isn't necessary

but, we found they inclined, without this top saturation, to turn yellow. Then if we snipped off the discoloration, the symmetry of the plant was destroyed. We are careful, too, not to cut off all the one-day-fresh blooms when they fade. Some of these must remain as a source of most welcome gift plants for our waiting list of friends, because the young plants grow out of the same spot as the bloom.

This progeny is allowed to develop in place until May. Then the young plants are cut off and separately potted. Although they are first launched with no roots at all, by autumn they form a fine cluster of their own, while the tops are likely to equal the height of the parents. Furthermore, they may even be ready with late winter blooms but more likely these will not occur until the second year. The usual soil mixture suits both youth and age. So, too, does plunging in the same semi-shaded location in the summer garden where extra watering is most essential if a fine winter future is to be expected.

When marica plants do not bloom fully, the answer is almost always *overpotting*. The large tops suggest the need of a large container. Actually the roots take up little space so a just-big-enough pot for these is proper rather than one in proportion to the fanned-out top.

Because it is so sturdy and fast growing, the marica often outgrows the smaller scaled window garden. Older plants are therefore frequently divided or else wisely discarded in favor of a younger generation. Repotting to larger quarters is an essential May chore for all year-old stock.

23. Some Favorite Oddments

THROUGH the years there have passed in and out of our window gardens certain minor characters, not important enough perhaps to be cast in major rôles but still meriting our affection or casual interest. Some last only a few weeks, others for those who want them, have permanent value.

The yellow Paris daisies or marguerites, *Chrysanthemum frutescens*, are favorites in this class. Just now we have two five-inch pots of them placed in a basket at the landing window. There are seven open blooms and a promise of long succession from a multitude of buds. Our visitor from the Canaries has ferny foliage and engaging yellow bloom which with a background of blue wall paper gives a gay greeting to all who mount and descend the stairs. The plants also offer an ever-present source of cut flowers in winter when they are most prized.

In our 68° F. house this marguerite seems to have but one demand: water. Before we realized the extent of its gigantic thirst, we could not understand the reason for discolored lower foliage. (As always, we felt put out to find a plant not liking us!) Now we know, it must for supreme contentment spend one full hour out of every twenty-four in a kitchen bowl filled with water to within an inch of its pot brim. So pampered, it flourishes in the manner of the Biblical green bay tree and offers a full year of charming color. Obtain it in November in bud and early bloom. It will flower all winter indoors and then in a sunny garden (an inverted peach basket for shade over it, please, for the first three days outside) continue in color until frost. This marguerite is a treasure which, as you see, we love to talk about.

There is also a blue marguerite, *Felicia amelloides*, which bears lovely sky blue flowers, thus offering an unusual color among the other house plants. Free blooming like the Paris daisy, it too is good for the long pull. Its cousin, *F. petiolata*, is attractive in hanging baskets. Both are scarce but now and then we find a florist who has a few of these beauties.

The Cinerarias are flowering plants which incline to make us nervous because of the violence of their purple, magenta and cerise hues. Somehow when we see them at flower shows or in florists' shops they always seem to have been placed by someone a trifle color blind. Actually there are paler pinks and whiter too while the deeper shades, if used alone, can be pleasing. Cinerarias as house plants have but a transient stay. With plenty of water, no sun, a circulation of air around them and a cool spot nearer 60° F. than 65° F. they are decorative at best for only a fortnight.

The pocketbook plant, or Calceolaria, comes with a multitude of red and yellow-spotted flowers each inflated like a little pouch. It is a pleasant novelty among gift plants but with a beauty span of only two or three weeks. At that the temperature must not be above 60° F. Therefore this is a plant not to buy for yourself unless practicalities are no object. If you receive it from a friend, keep it watered well as you do your marguerites, and consider it as one of life's briefer blessings.

A plant the florist almost never carries is *Impatiens sultani*, the familiar name of which, oddly enough, is Patience Plant. He doesn't include it in his careful calculations because it is so easy to grow that without benefit of greenhouse and simply by slips it spreads over whole neighborhoods and has even passed down through generations. Pieces broken off the parent plant root with no attention at all in a glass of water while mature plants bloom as lustily as wax begonias in light or in sunshine.

The old-fashioned patience plant produced little highlights of red or rose all over its fresh green growth. Today there are impatiens hybrids of pink, violet and white as well as red and the succulent foliage is often variegated. Ancestor and offspring are alike, however, in having good dispositions and a tendency to take philosophically the indoor world as they find it. Plenty of moisture is a basic, imperative need without which this gay and obliging little window plant cannot endure.

After flowering enthusiastically all winter it may be trimmed back a little to shapeliness in late spring and spend its summer plunged in partial shade in the garden. There it will continue to bloom vigorously. This is one of the easiest plants to grow from seed sown outdoors in pots in May. By late summer the bright little blooms begin to appear.

The Flowering Maple, *Abutilon*, with its crêpe paper bells of red, yellow or white, is another flower to call forth memories. This is not a narrow shelf subject but a glorious bay window filler, shapely and handsome when in maturity it has the form of a miniature maple tree and the nicely shaped leaf as well.

A forehanded enthusiast with a whole sunroom to fill in winter would have fun raising a lusty crop of abutilons from spring-sown seed. Grown along as pot plants and frequently pinched to make them shapely, these would reach a three- to four-foot size before the outside growing season ended. Then they would be equal to a big decorating rôle in the winter with first and thereafter continuous flowers from late February on.

Indoors with ample sunshine, water and more than usual emphasis on ventilation, these century-old favorites bloom constantly. If in the neighborhood a specimen of this flowering maple already exists, you can easily start a more restricted number of plants or just one from stem cuttings taken at any time and rooted in water or sand.

The sweetness of Heliotrope brings to all who have loved gardens the fragrance of the past. Because it is such a beautiful treasure we wish we could urge you all to include it among your house plants. Unfortunately, it seems more than other plants to be dependent on greenhouse conditions and besides it almost invariably harbors white fly.

However, if you are one of the optimists who can cater successfully to a gardenia, it may be you can manage the exacting heliotrope as well. If you can procure a plant from the florist, make up your mind to employ every possible device for humidifying the air.

Or the heliotrope which has adorned your outdoor

garden may be the object of your energies. Often such plants have possibilities and continue to bloom through the fall and into the winter. Outdoor heliotrope is dug early in September with as little root disturbance as possible and potted in soil rich in humus and with a little added plant food. (If some commercial garden mixture is at hand, allow one teaspoon to a five-inch pot.)

After several shaded days to allow for transplanting shock, the heliotrope is again introduced to longer and longer periods of sun until, without wilting, it can again endure a constantly sunny exposure. Meanwhile, soil is freely watered and the foliage syringed daily.

Before a hint of frost, the heliotrope is moved to a sunny window but in a spot with a temperature reliably below 60° F. Be mindful about fresh air the first weeks and try daily to syringe the tops or else to hold them under a faucet with the plant turned on its side so the soil will not be overly saturated.

Since it is a tender perennial, the heliotrope can in this way frequently be held over from year to year. If you crave both work and heliotrope, such is the method. If you prefer the emphasis to be on heliotrope alone, buy young budded florist's plants in the fall and go all out for humidity.

24. Orchids Are Not Impossible

WOULD an orchid plant costing approximately the amount of a two-flower corsage strike you as a bargain?

Then by all means plan to join the circle which includes a lawyer who grows orchids in a 14th floor New York apartment, a housewife in New Jersey in a bay window, a steam fitter on a window sill in Brooklyn and the captain of an ocean liner in his cabin. Glamorous as they always will be to residents of the temperate zone, orchids can come into the kitchen or whichever room you prefer, providing the right varieties are selected.

Not every kind of orchid is a good investment for room culture. Most satisfactory are the Cypripedium or Slipper Orchids. Surely you have noticed them in florist windows, lovely waxen blooms with the lower petal like a slipper. Yellow, green, brown and white, sometimes flecked or spotted, flowers are long-lasting and the plants of easy culture. The New York enthusiast for example, had the crisp green and white Cypripedium Maudiae open one February 17. It was still fresh enough to pick for a festive occasion one month later.

Certain varieties of the showy Cattleya, of which we all think whenever orchids are mentioned, can also be grown. *C. Trianae* is one of the best for winter flowering. Cymbidium, however, are our favorites. Their blossoms are similar in shape but smaller than cattleyas and are poised on a long stem like so many enormous, hovering butterflies. And the colors are just as soft and delicately blended.

These three groups of orchids are enough for a start; future acquisitions more unusual in color and form may be purchased upon the advice of an orchid grower once your intelligent approach to growing them at home has been proven. It is not wise to pick up any orchid plant anywhere. If you are serious about growing them in a window garden, make friends with a reputable orchid man and be guided by his advice on the kinds to choose and their culture. In the long run it pays to buy mature, well established plants rather than the less expensive seedlings which may not bloom for years.

Orchid plants can be overwatered, permitted too much sunshine, kept too cold or too hot. Light, heat, humidity and air must all be watched carefully. They do need light but full burning sun is undesirable. Thus in the sunny south or west window a thin curtain or some means of shading is necessary even in winter.

Overwatering is the most common error of novices. Nothing is more deadly to a healthy orchid plant, even excess moisture from the syringing of the foliage. Ordinarily a good drenching, once a week, of the osmundine fiber in which they grow is sufficient. Sometimes in clear warm weather, they'll need to be watered twice a week or even three times in summer. A fine syringing of the foliage every day is helpful but this must be fine enough to evaporate and not leave drops on the foliage to start leaf spot.

A temperature that does not fall below 55° F. at night nor over 70° F. by day is ideal. The orchid family is such a varied one that many kinds can be grown within this range and the exact temperature for each depends upon the plant itself and the humidity furnished in its situation.

Some practical method of supplying humidity must be

found for without it orchids cannot grow and flower. At this point trays re-enter the picture and we may safely recommend this as one plant that can be grown over a radiator. Metal trays or pans three inches deep, half filled with clean pebbles or stone chips, are covered with a rack made of thin wooden slats spaced about one-half inch apart. On this are set the potted orchids. The stones are kept wet to supply humidity and a further aid will be large containers of water behind or on top of the radiator. Of course humidifiers may be purchased or your home may be air-conditioned!

As a final precaution, plants are so placed on the rack as to allow circulation of air. Orchids like fresh air and need a little every day not as a draught but from opening a window the veriest crack during midday. Plants are never to be fertilized. In addition to daily spraying and watering whenever necessary, the weekly going over includes washing the leaves and a thorough hunt for scale. Nothing so encourages this scourge as cold and dampness — beware! Care and well regulated surroundings mean little, if any, trouble.

It's not easy to grow orchids, for no house provides ideal conditions without some adjustments. Once you have had a single plant flower and lend its exotic touch to the window garden, you'll be ready to delve into other mysteries of orchid growing, division of the original plant, "back bulbs", and potting. We warn you that orchids are not easy on your budget because a catalogue is so enticingly filled with many names and romantic descriptions. But we say once more — trust your dealer —

and when you have followed his advice, purchasing the plants he recommends and settling them in your home, you may be surprised to discover that they are no harder and a lot less constant care than a great many ordinary house plants.

25. The Poinsettia Has More Than a Past

THE poinsettia which on December 25 brings you the brightest greetings of the season is all too likely by January 1 to suggest only gruesome possibilities for the coming year. With green leaves already fallen and red bracts deteriorating, it no longer has decorative qualities of any kind. Even a carefully planned future may not offset the ill effects of its obviously unpleasant recent experience.

Yet this need not be so. Indeed, with careful nurture, our own poinsettias have sometimes lasted so long into March that they began to acquire an embalmed, otherworld appearance, and we have summarily retired them in the interests of variety.

For fairly prolonged decoration in the window garden, the single stem plants in three- or four-inch pots are the most useful and far easier to care for properly than those odd traditional combinations of fern and poinsettia plants which were never meant to be so intimate, since ferns want one kind of life and poinsettias require another. Small specimens in Christmas red, white or a lovely soft dusty rose pink offer possibilities for regrouping — at the foreground for the holidays and to the side thereafter.

Poinsettias maintain both leaves and looks if, as soon as they arrive from the florist, they are placed in a light window when the temperature is steady — about 65° F. in the daytime and not lower than 60° F. at night — and where there is protection from draughts. It is high heat, sudden chilling and dry atmosphere which cause immediate havoc. An easy way to increase humidity is to keep water in the saucers in which the plants stand, with each pot resting on a level layer of pebbles and so held above and not in direct contact with moisture. Soil is watered enough to keep it barely damp, neither soggy nor dry. For plants in very small containers, this often means twice daily. Hot, dry rooms will also necessitate the double watering.

When finally — and finally should certainly not be before February — the leaves turn yellow, water is gradually withheld (but ferns if present are first separately potted) and the dry plant in a few weeks time stored until spring at 60° F. In May it is brought again to the sun, cut back to six inches, shaken free of old soil and returned to its former container, or one just a size larger. There with the regular pleasing soil mixture firmed about its roots, it is thoroughly watered. Very soon vigorous four- to six-inch lengths of new growth develop.

These can be immediately pruned off, the cut ends dipped for a moment in very hot water to check the oozing of sap, and then separately inserted two inches deep in small pots of warm moist sand which is carefully firmed around the stems. A drinking glass inverted over each cutting inspires more enthusiastic rooting because the illusion develops that greenhouse conditions have been provided, even though it is still only the kitchen or parlor.

When roots are well formed (pull up a cutting after three weeks to see what goes on. You can tuck it back again without damage) the young plants are transferred to three-inch pots (or set three to a seven-inch pan) containing the usual soil. After all danger of frost is over and nights are warm, the poinsettias, old and young, are plunged for a refreshing holiday in a fairly sunny garden bed.

There in August overlong new branches on older plants are pruned to hold back flowering for the holidays (although it may not be possible to time it exactly for Christmas as the florist does). When a large plant is the ultimate aim, top and sides are trimmed back less than a third. For a center-of-the-table kind of plant all but three or five shoots, depending on available growth, are cut out entirely and the rest trimmed to within two inches of old wood. Thus your view of Uncle Tom or Cousin Kate consuming turkey opposite is in no way impeded by a towering poinsettia!

During garden months the poinsettia with its restricted root room is often in need of extra watering between showers of rain. A refreshing syringing of the tops with the hose is a good thing anyway. Then because of its tropical nature it is whisked indoors before autumn nights turn cool and check its flowering ardor. Inside at the sunniest possible window, but still no warmer than 65° F., the plant is fed every two weeks in November and December, with a little liquid manure or a dissolved plant tablet, according to the manufacturer's directions.

And always a close atmosphere is avoided. Especially is fresh air important during the first weeks indoors when the contrast between the humid open garden and dry house air so often results in a resentful shedding of leaves. Whenever fresh air is admitted during cold weather, however, it must come indirectly so as to be of proper temperature. Chills for a poinsettia inevitably result in its own unattractive version of the common cold.

26. Primroses Have a Delicate Air

STANDBY of the florist shop from January through March are primroses, typified to most of us by large-leaved, stocky plants topped with chunky clusters of rose or lavender bloom. A passing glance rather than mounting excitement is their lot, particularly since the foliage when handled produces on many persons a rash similar to poison ivy. But there is much more to the primrose story than this *Primula obconica*.

These same three months of the year bring into flower the Baby or Fairy Primroses, *Primula malacoides*. Tall stems encircled not once but two or three times with dainty little blooms, each one rather like a forget-me-not, surmount the plants with a white or lavender mist. They are so nice to cut that it is fortunate they are produced freely. And incidentally, faded blossoms should be snipped off immediately in order to sustain a three-month flowering period.

And then there are the Chinese Primroses, *P. sinensis*, which rate the house plant society columns. Best known is Dazzler, a floriferous sunset red variety belonging to the fringed group, *P. sinensis fimbriata*. Of all the primroses, our favorites are *P. sinensis stellata*, and of all the colors in this star group, Salmon Beauty or Coral Pink Star is the most irresistible. The name speaks for the flowers, and we cannot do without it.

Primroses are adaptable plants for the three deadly winter months. A dozen of the white fairy primroses scattered over the pebble-filled tray of one of our window gardens makes it fresh as a spring zephyr, and they last much longer. Quite by accident one day, we dropped two plants in a little wicker basket. The effect delighted us so that now, in season, the basket is kept filled and is moved all over the house: dressing up a table in the guest room for the weekend, later cheering the family at the breakfast table, and ending its days in the sitting room. Coral Pink Star, either singly or in groups, never fails in creating beauty.

No matter which of the three primroses you may have, their home life follows the same pattern. Lots of light, plenty of water and a cool temperature are vital necessities. A hot, dry room shortens a primrose career by weeks. An east or west window, where the sun filters in briefly and gently is perfect. The sunny south window provides too strong light. Presumably primroses do best in a temperature of 45 to 50° F. but unless there is a sunporch where the radiator can be turned off during the day, this is almost impossible. Frankly, ours have completed a long and lovely flowering span in a temperature reaching the low sixties.

At any temperature, water, frequent and plentiful, is required. The primrose is another plant which must stand in a saucer, for unless it is watered from the bottom, foliage must be lifted each time to keep moisture from the center of the plant. Besides top watering is likely to be insufficient. A deep saucer and watering twice daily is important since primrose roots do not take kindly to constant moisture.

Primrose plants are hardly worth saving for a second year of bloom, although it can be done, most successfully perhaps with the Chinese primrose. New plants flower better and, if your budget won't permit the number you'd like to have, a whole flock can be raised from seed. That is, if you're patient and careful. The seed sowing schedule runs like this to get flowering plants next January: *P. obconica* and *P. malacoides* are sown March to June, *P. sinensis*, April to August.

We usually start seeds in a bulb pan, sunk in the coldframe or in the coldframe itself, preparing a mixture of half sand and soil. The planting is kept moist but not wet, shaded and cool. When seedlings have two pairs of true primrose leaves, transplanting begins. The first one makes a row of plants spaced an inch apart in the coldframe, the second one places each plant in its own individual pot, and probably two more shiftings will be necessary until by September each plant respectably fills a four-inch pot. Before freezing weather, usually in early November, the young huskies are brought indoors and kept in the coolest possible place until there are signs of flower buds. Feeding with liquid manure is done monthly once the pot stage is reached and increased to fortnightly doses when the plants are brought indoors.

27. Southern Nostalgia

WHETHER or not we go to Florida in winter, there is always a bit of the south at one of our windows. Trying to cope with the gardenia is not necessary if one can obtain jasmine. Sometimes the gardenia is called the cape jessamine or jasmine but we would feel lost without the climbing Spanish or Catalonian variety, *Jasminum grandiflorum*. It makes a lacy green curtain at one of our south windows all winter, for the long stiff stems bear pairs of small fine-cut leaves. In late winter, starry white flowers with a heavenly perfume begin to appear.

This jasmine is the easiest of plants to grow. It likes both sun and warmth although in a hot dry room, red spider may begin its deadly attack. A vigorous cool shower once a week holds this in check. In summer the jasmine will do well in partial shade and ours is plunged pot and all close to the fence where it will have some support for climbing.

The jasmine does not outgrow its five-inch pot, for this size container accommodates a root system sufficient for the top growth which is pruned back every fall. At this time its resting period begins. Dead wood is trimmed out and old stems cut back to stimulate fresh growth for next year's blossoms. During the autumn months the plant, though indoors, is kept as cool as possible (40 to 55° F. is best) and watered sparingly. By New Year's signs of new life appear, the jasmine returns to its sunny window, is watered daily and fertilized with liquid manure once a fortnight.

Still another of these fragrant Southern vines is the Confederate Jasmine, *Trachelospermum jasminoides*, which is so well-behaved that after ten years our plant can still be regarded as a standard rather than a climber. Slender bamboo stakes support its fairly constant eighteen-inch height. Every February, however, waxy fragrant white flowers accentuate the sheer romance of its name.

Confederate jasmine warrants the sunniest spot in the window garden, and does best in a temperature that does not exceed 65° F. The regular monthly watering with liquid manure is increased to twice monthly after New Year's as its flowering season approaches. By May, however, the flower orgy has passed and the somewhat leathery green leaves begin to fall, indicating the plant's yearning for summer vacation. It is then repotted in fresh soil and plunged in a semi-shaded garden spot.

The exquisite Camellia is still another Southern possibility if — and this is a big if — you have a cool enough location. It is too much the conservatory or cool greenhouse plant to take kindly to the hot and dry living room. Also it is too large a plant to fit into the window garden but if you have a cool sunporch or even a cool bedroom with a sunny window, the camellia is a long-lived plant whose flowering will be something worth calling in the neighbors to see.

Camellia japonica is an evergreen shrub which is hardy as far north as Charleston, South Carolina. The dark green leaves are extremely decorative; the flat round flowers with many overlapping petals, so evenly arranged, are perfection itself. White, shades of pink, carmine and red or white splotched with color are so lovely that not even their complete lack of fragrance detracts from their charm.

While camellias must be grown cool as a house plant, they cannot stand draughts nor near freezing temperatures. At night 45 to 50° F. is their limit while day temperatures of 50 to 60° F. are best. Some growers say a constant 50° F. is most favorable; others that with humidity, the plants can stand as much as 65° F. during the day. Since nothing within this range will kill camellias, you can soon learn which extremes are most favorable with the other conditions in your home. Frequent syringing helps to maintain a humid atmosphere.

During early winter the plants are not watered excessively, perhaps every other day. But as soon as flower buds form, more warmth and heat are needed. Each watering should soak the ball of roots and the plant should not be watered again while the soil is still wet. When buds begin to show, it's time to start watering with liquid manure. A loose peaty soil is the camellia's specialty, a mixture of garden loam, peatmoss or leafmold and sand in equal proportions.

Camellias reach full flowering in March, and each

blossom lasts a fairly long time. After bloom is over, increased heat encourages new growth. At this time the plants can be repotted if necessary but they prefer a tight fit. In June when nights no longer are chill, camellias may go outdoors in a semi-shaded place. The real rest period is in fall after they have been brought back into the house but these quiet months are worth while in return for the few spring weeks of lovely bloom.

28. Special Enchantment

PROBABLY we enjoy our south window garden most in October when the lavender blue masses of *Plumbago capensis* sway gently on their wand-like stems and blend with the pink bouvardia in perfect companionship. Charming as this picture is, it is not difficult to bring into being, nor is it shortlived, for the plumbago flowers for two months in the fall and the bouvardia from October to February.

Plumbago is one of our treasures. Several years ago when it first came from the florist the four-inch pot fitted the kerosene lamp bracket at one side of the window. But alas, this plumbago is a vine which has increased in length and breadth with every summer until now nothing less than an eight-inch pot will accommodate it. (This means it stands on the floor.) A slender trellis supports the graceful green stems which extend the height of the window frame. It is difficult to steel ourselves each September to prune back its lush green growth to something approaching house size. Thinning out and shortening stems proves worth while when the burst of delicate bloom appears in the fall and again from January to April.

No other plant so personifies spring, for it seems as though the blue phlox which flowers outdoors with the tulips in May have suddenly jumped into the window garden. A white variety is also known. The clusters of periwinkle blue blossoms are produced in a soft tuft at the ends of the stems, bending them over ever so gracefully.

Plumbago is far from temperamental. It likes all possible sunshine so a south window, unshaded, is required. Daily watering is also needed by so large a plant and the weekly shower bath keeps it fresh in appearance. It will do best in a temperature of 55 to 65° F. though slight variations at either extreme do not trouble it, providing humidity and moisture are maintained. The plant is fertilized once every four weeks during its indoor stay. By the time spring bloom has petered out, plumbago is ready, and looks it, for the rest, which the garden can provide. And so the plant is repotted in fresh soil, and plunged outdoors where it will be shaded and protected from strong winds.

Three pots of pink bouvardia fill the window sill beneath the plumbago. We prefer the pink because the flowers are somewhat smaller and finer in texture than the white, to say nothing of being a most entrancing shade of coral. But either white or pink ones are worth the farthest search and whatever cajoling is necessary to make a greenhouse owner part with two or three plants.

Established specimens, about ready to form buds in September, are easy to bring into handsome maturity. They, too, like maximum sun and repay generously in flowers for monthly feeding. Truth to tell, they can stand more heat than plumbago, although 55 to 65° F. will be ideal. Daily watering is advisable to maintain flowering and a weekly syringing absolutely necessary if red spider is not to attack the plant. But ours have survived that hazard and in spite of a mild infestation have continued to flower.

By New Year's, it will seem as though your pink bouvardia simply cannot stop producing buds and you may wish that, after all, you had chosen the white ones. Once the last flowers have faded, these plants are finished save to provide cuttings for next winter's display. Stem cuttings are not too difficult to root and may then be potted into a humusy soil mixture and shifted to larger pots as they grow. They are brought along in the coldframe during the summer for well established plants by September.

To complete a triumvirate of dainty flowers, Sweet Olive, *Olea fragrans*, should also be in the south window. The tiny clusters of even tinier white flowers are sweetly fragrant, especially on a bright day when their scent is unforgettable and pungent. The first ones of the season are as certain a signal of Thanksgiving as cranberry sauce and turkey. Starting in late November, a sweet olive blooms steadily and profusely until it is transferred to the garden in June for an enforced vacation.

The oval leaves, dark green and somewhat leathery, are those of an evergreen. Perhaps that is why sweet olive does not grow too rapidly. A shift in pot sizes is not necessary oftener than every two years, although the plants are repotted in fresh soil each June before they are placed under the cut-leaf maple.

Sweet olive has extremely good manners all winter. Ours has never attracted an insect during all of six years. Daily watering, weekly syringing and monthly feeding are the sum total of its attention, after sun and a location guaranteeing 55 to 68° F. have been found. It is possible to go far without matching the permanency or continuous bloom of sweet olive. Together or alone, breathtaking plumbago, brilliant bouvardia and demure sweet olive can make the south window a place of special enchantment.

29. Succulents, Our Own Selection

UNDER the pompous and unimaginative classification of succulents are included some of the most delightful and undemanding house plants of all. If you attempt to select these from a catalogue, their names will very likely slay you, but if you follow our example and hie to a grower where masses of these charmers are grown, you will find yourself so captivated by odd bits of color and delicate sprays of bloom that names like *Echeveria secunda glauca* or *Mesembryanthemum deltoides* cannot rise up to put you off.

It is plants of this kind as well as sedums, gasterias,

haworthias, kleinias and opuntias, which in spite of their nomenclature, we have so often selected to arrange in one dish as a garden by itself for a coffee table. We have also chosen from among these when we have wanted for a quite small window, material not likely soon to outgrow its quarters. We have found that so long as we grow these various succulents quite dry, they have done a nice decorative job for us, most of them keeping their small tidy forms and not needing repotting for several years. Besides variety in form, there has been surprising contrast in color of foliage while occasional little spots of bloom have added a bit of bright coral or red, sometimes even a daisy-like purple.

Some succulents in more important sizes are also valuable. In one garden on an upper shelf we spaced an aloe and a bold columnar *Euphorbia lactea* for silhouettes high up against the light. And then like almost all other window gardeners in the course of years we have developed great affection for such reliables as the jade plant *Crassula arborescens*, the crown-of-thorns *Euphorbia splendens*, and the kalanchoes which seem to us excellent red and green rivals of the poinsettia.

* * * *

This Crassula, sometimes called the Japanese rubber plant or jade tree, came to us in a two-inch pot but in the course of ten years beautifully developed its natural tree-like form, and at about three feet became of a size for tub culture. It even took to blooming in the early spring and was a lovely sight when adorned with its aura of fragrant white blossoms. This is an almost never-fail plant although it has to be well matured and highly content to offer a bouquet. It does well in either a light or sunny place and in the average soil mixture with a shift to a one size larger pot about every other May.

Adequate drainage arrangement, plenty of fresh air and not too much water constitute the happy life for the jade plant. If leaves drop or growth gets either lanky or soft some one of these three essential aspects of culture is in question. Usually letting the plant dry out thoroughly, extending the period of daily fresh air and pinching back overlong shoots will put it right again.

When the plant is little it needs water about every other day, perhaps every day if the sun is bright but as it attains size, the water storing nature of its leaves makes so much moisture unnecessary. Once or twice a week is enough for the four-inch pot size while our tubbed adult now wants a good soaking but once in ten days. (At the same time to keep the foliage fresh, we syringe it lightly about twice a month, keeping the plant out of the sun until it dries.)

Especially during the resting period must watering be slight and the temperature cool. This time lasts for two to three months and usually occurs from about September to December. You can spot it because fresh growth ceases and the plant for a long time maintains a status quo not to be interrupted by overzealous watering and feeding.

In May repotting is avoided if possible because the

roots are so resentful of disturbance but the top soil in the pot can be scooped out a little and some fresh garden loam plus bone meal worked in as a refresher. Then the plant is placed on the porch out of the wind and in the shade. At this time new little jade plants are easily started by pressing three- or four-inch cuttings from the parent stock into a pot of damp sandy soil.

* * * *

The special blessing of the Crown of Thorns is that it is almost never out of bloom. Indeed, the constant productiveness of this thorny twiner never ceases to amaze us as week after week and month after month its bright red flower clusters shine out amid inch-long thorns and small bright green leaves.

Full sun, a tight container and rather sandy soil on the dry side with an open air summer in semi-shade constitute its modest requirements. To keep it from being a bramble thicket we train it early to the support of a small trellis or a curved wire coat hanger. (Such a gadget is nice for other twiners too, we find. First we straighten and then curve the wires as we wish, finally inserting them into the soil by the flattened out hook end.)

* * * *

Only recently have those grand succulents, the kalanchoes of Africa appeared in the shops. If at Christmas the coral ardisia strains your purse and the crimson poinsettia, from your past experiences, hates you on sight, try these rose, scarlet or crimson-flowering plants with their ruddy, fleshy leaves and tendency to keep on with repeated blooms from November or December to May. *Kalanchoe coccinea* (you pronounce it Kal-an-koh'ee but the florist attacks it various ways) and *K. carnea*, which is fragrant, are kinds easily procured.

We could perhaps be fancy about culture but actually like most succulents these want little here below — full sun, a rather dry condition though more water during the growing season, a gritty soil and semi-shade in summer. Also, fresh air is essential. One year our plants were frightfully attacked by mealy bug which we blamed primarily on inadequate ventilation. However, we cleaned that up fast not with the traditional wood alcohol, because none could be bought, that season, but by dipping our swabs in a readily available Christmas present — some "Blue Grass" toilet water which our kalanchoes seem to like as much as we do!

30. These Are Choice Extras

LIKE petunias and marigolds in the borders, the indoor garden has its standbys of geranium and begonia. But in time constant success with these easy subjects creates a desire for something new. It is then that a number of relatively unknown greenhouse plants offer a special challenge to the enthusiast who fancies an interesting experience or two.

There's the exotic flamingo flower, *Anthurium scherzerianum*, for example. Our first thought was that such a charmer from the lily family would never consent to our average home life. But behold it took to us at once, and remained happy for years. (This was a satisfaction, since its purchase set us back a bit at the outset.)

We selected a coral red variety and hoped to enjoy an occasional bloom. Almost constant color from our anthurium was therefore a grand surprise. Indeed, our plant diary for 1936 indicates that except for a brief resting period between June 13 and August 23 there was always a flamingo flower in some stage of development, and although the number was limited, each lasted long. Thus one bud, first visible on March 16, opened so slowly and then stayed fresh so long, that the matured flower did not fade completely until June 10 — practically a three-months' performance.

And how fascinating is that slow and deliberate process of florescence. The flower begins as a twisted cone, gradually changing into a rather flat formation with a spike or spadix at first almost knotted, and silhouetted by a petal-like spathe. Later the spike straightens out and the spathe turns down below it. We then supply a slender bamboo stake to display and support the new bloom.

Cream white, crimson-spotted and many blush rose and red varieties exist. Such plants, of course, are not to be picked up at every corner though very often your local florist can obtain one for you from one of the larger growers.

But flowers are not the only asset of anthurium. Those narrow, shining evergreen leaves are attractive too and almost completely disease and pest resistant. In three years time ours had to have but one soapy bath to clean up some aphids. Of course, the leaves were regularly cleansed with water to keep them dust free.

Other cultural essentials include plenty of sunlight, and copious watering except during periods of rest or of completed bloom. Once a flower is perfected the plant seems to need much less water than while it is working on it. Then when the bloom fades, resting ceases (unless it is summer vacation time) and more moisture is immediately needed again. The pebble-saucer device is helpful in promoting humidity and we provide a 70° F. temperature with little drop at night.

Between flowerings we remove some of the top soil and replace it with flower bed soil to which extra bone meal and some sheep manure (one teaspoon of each per five-inch pot of soil) has been added.

Repotting is put off as long as possible since root disturbance is not at all to the liking of this plant of settled habit. When more root room becomes essential, however, very adequate drainage arrangements are made in the larger pot and some sphagnum moss (the florist will supply a few handfuls if you haven't any saved from the packing of rose bushes or shrubs sent through the mail) or other coarse humus material mixed in the soil. Near the end of January is often a good time for a shift or else just before the plunging of the anthurium in the relatively sunny garden in June.

At this point we can not forbear mention of a more sedate cousin of the flamingo flower. Alas, it has no common name and so we present *Spathiphyllum flori-*

bundum. It has the same fascinating florescence, chalk white, which lasts for an unbelievably long time and gathers a greenish tinge as it ages.

Our "calla lily" as some friends call this far more fragile appearing bloom, sometimes courageously pokes out a bud in February, but the blooms are more likely to be numbered among the Easter plants.

The rest of the year it is an admirable foliage plant. Sometimes during winter we cannot resist cutting a few leaves for flower arrangements. It is one of those good plants, content to serve in the background for the greater part of the year but well deserving a prominent spot when the flowers appear.

Save for repotting, which is best timed in June, the care of spathiphyllum dovetails with that of the flamingo flower. It doesn't take kindly to either repotting or division so once in three or four years is enough. Liquid manure used monthly from November to May, encourages flower development and plant growth.

*   *   *   *

Another bird-like flower is borne by *Strelitzia reginae*, the glowing orange and purple bird-of-paradise plant. Maturity is a prime factor in the brilliant March to May display of this South African plant of the banana family. Hence it costs a pretty penny because the grower has to tend it so long before it reaches blooming size in six- to seven-inch pots.

We took ours off his hands one spring at the four-inch size and patiently hovered over it for a whole year. Then came our glorious reward in the astounding form of the tropical flowers. However, even as a foliage plant our strelitzia was good to look at.

And time has taught us its requirements. Richer than average diet is agreeable so whenever the plant is unfurling leaves or developing buds we are at hand every fortnight to administer, around the outer edge of the well moistened soil, a few tablespoonfuls of liquid manure. But when from September to the end of November it indicates that a rest cure is in order we place it in the cold, but never freezing, sunroom away from light and with a low supply of water. As new leaves appear in December, we bring it again to full sun and warmth, that is to 70° F., and water and feed it freely. We feel that even one flower is a fair dividend while the possible six or eight of a well satisfied strelitzia is an event well worth taking trouble. As the plants develop considerable size, we shift them from pots to tubs and in summer place them on the porch where some morning sun can reach them.

* * * *

Likewise a brilliant traveler from South Africa is *Clivia miniata*. This is an amaryllis-like beauty with the habit of year-round growth so that it is always attractive. It needs about a 40° F. winter resort rest from December to February, while it gathers energy for its late winter and spring pageant and through these weeks it is held on the dry side.

When finally around March the clivia comes across

with those glowing umbels of rich orange red, every cluster containing ten to twenty gorgeous individual blossoms and each one two inches across, we positively hate to leave it alone in the house. It looks like something valuable enough for a special insurance policy and it keeps up its expensive appearance for two weeks or more.

We found such grandeur was dependent on a settled condition and a rich diet, so all the time the clivia isn't resting we spoon on the liquid manure, just as we do for the strelitzia. We repot only about once in three years and then with the greatest care just after the flowering season. It seems best, too, at that time to step up the fertility of the usual soil mixture with a third instead of a quarter of old manure and to double the bone meal quota.

After repotting we practically turn handsprings to increase humidity so that the plant will quickly start growth again and produce a lot of new acclimating roots in its new quarters. Daily spraying until it goes to summer quarters on the porch seems the best plan and a warm room to stimulate new lush growth. (Incidentally when the plant is being grown warm, the mealy bug plus relatives is inclined to move in, so be ready with plenty of alcohol dipped swabs.)

*   *   *   *

If you've taken up the Mexican trend in decoration, the Shrimp Plant, *Beloperone guttata*, is appropriate. After all, it is a native Mexican and one which makes itself completely comfortable in a sunny window. We have had plants no more than three inches tall flower and the distinctively colored, queer little sheaves of bloom may be fairly constant from November until April.

Like the poinsettia, the shrimp plant has not true flowers but an inflorescence in which bracts supply the muted color. Two-lipped white blossoms protrude from the short overlapping bracts whose color and form evidently reminded someone of a shrimp. They droop gracefully against the small green leaves.

"Attractive, clean and vigorous house plant" is the catalogue's modest description. To that should be added easy-going. Give the shrimp plant sun, plenty of water and the regular soil mixture, and it will take care of itself. Small plants rooted from cuttings in late summer have grown as much as three inches a month in a sunny south window.

Shrimp plants have a tendency to become tall and skinny by spring so the summer vacation is welcome for the chance to transfer them to the garden. If they are planted in a sunny part of the flower border, the stems cut back, and the plants not stinted for water, better shaped specimens will grow to flowering size there and be ready to be potted up for the indoor garden in autumn. Cuttings three or four inches long root easily in sand for new plants. Once you obtain a shrimp plant by fair means or foul, it will never give you any cause for being without one again.

All of these plants are sufficiently exotic to demand a

special setting. In fact, if you don't give it to them, they'll make wherever they are just that. The window garden, where neither the flowers nor their color will go unnoticed, accommodates flamingo flower and shrimp plant. But the spaciousness of a sunroom is better suited to the glowing hues and size of clivia and strelitzia. These are glamour queens too sophisticated for touching leaves daily with a Boston fern or an aspidistra and elegant enough to dominate even the drawing room.

31. Trailers and Climbers for Color

TALL or dwarf, erect or trailing, climbing or creeping — every sort of plant has its part to play in the staging of a window garden. Proud as we may be of home-grown primroses, second year poinsettias or the glossy holly fern, several of the trailing plants serve a purpose that none of these standards can fulfil. These trailers on brackets at either side of the window or arranged along the sill break the outline in a soft and pleasing manner. They are also interesting enough to be used as specimen plants wherever such a decorative item is appropriate.

Asparagus fern, A. *sprengeri*, which isn't a fern at all, is one of the softest and most luxuriant of green plants. That is, if it is well grown. It makes no special demands for either soil or water but prefers an east or west window where light rather than sunlight prevails. Should the mass of slender stems encircled with needle-like green leaves begin to yellow, it is a signal of too much heat or sun.

More colorful but not so graceful is Anthericum or Spider Plant. The small new ones which may hang as much as two feet below their parent might possibly remind you of giant spiders but what harmless ones! The narrow leaves are all green or striped with white just as is the main plant. Even the apartment house dweller can grow this on a shelf in the window, or on a bracket or bookcase.

No mean contribution for such unassuming plants is the color which several of these trailing ones furnish. Coleus, for example, has the finest of colored foliage, its leaves soft as velvet and tinted with rose or red or yellow, and as variously cut as they are tinted. Like anything gay, it needs all the sunlight it can get. Although it flourishes in water or in soil, the coleus likes room to spread and lift its arm-like stems. And it definitely resents too much water either because soil is poorly drained or the caretaker has spilled a few drops on the leaves.

Hardier than either of these are the dainty clover-like oxalis and the strawberry begonia. Goodness knows why this name was bestowed on *Saxifraga sarmentosa*. There is a rosy undertone to the leaves and stems that could pass for a strawberry color but neither the thin stems of white blossoms nor the scalloped round leaves resemble begonias. No friendlier plant exists for every spring slender pink runners (ah, yes, the strawberry part of the name) arch from the base of the plant and at their tips appear minute replicas of the parent. If the strawberry begonia rests on the pebble tray base of the window garden, these little fellows will take root and may soon be severed to start their own career. Or they may be pinched off and potted in soil. But don't expect strawberry begonias to act this way all year round. During fall and early winter they are quiescent, a mound of decorative foliage.

Oxalis blossom every sunny winter day from bulbs which have been planted in autumn. They need no root-

ing period to urge growth nor do they rest once the shamrock-like leaves and first pink or yellow blossoms start. Oxalis likes town or country and refuses to differentiate between apartment or mansion. It becomes a spreading, fluffy mat of green anywhere and only requires an occasional trimming of the yellowed leaves and blossoms.

Sophisticated window gardeners outgrow the brittle, small-leaved tradescantia. Like many other trailing plants, it is a colorful clan, for there is a simple green one, a variegated leaf type that grown in the sun may surprise you with tiny blue or lavender blossoms and a stunning large one, *Zebrina pendulosa*, with purple and silver-striped foliage. These are all too effective in little vases of colored glass or for creeping over pebbles to be scorned as common.

One other trailer, *Campanula isophylla*, famed for its starry blue and white flower cups, we hope to add to our garden some day. It will go on the bracket in the south window and if we can manage enough humidity, it will grow as handsomely as the plants we once saw in New Hampshire. Cuttings root easily, so they say, but plants are difficult to obtain from seed.

Meanwhile, we content ourselves with flowers from two honest-to-goodness vines, not trailers. One is the old-fashioned wax plant, *Hoya carnosa*. Lovely as are the fragrant clusters of tiny white blossoms with pink centers and brown eyes, the plant even out of bloom is beautiful all year. For the foliage is a constant medley of pink, white and green. As the waxy pointed leaves unfold, their color scheme is green and pink, later fading to white.

The slow-growing wax plant will in ten years time become a mass of six- to eight-foot stems reaching from any bracket toward the floor. That is, if it is left to grow twelve months of the year in a sunny east or west window, untouched save for an annual spring repotting and the weekly syringing with warm water. Until a considerable degree of maturity is reached, it will not bloom.

When the passion vine flowers on a bleak winter's day, we are so proud that neighbors must come and see this strangest of all blossoms. Ten creamy white petals surmounted with a blue filament are always an object of wonder. The large five-lobed green leaves and tightly coiled tendrils are decorative in themselves and a new foliage pattern among a galaxy of house plants.

The passion vine is a valued plant. Every year before frost we cut long stems from the garden plant in case a severe winter destroys it. These stems, so ornamental in a glass bowl, root quickly and may then be potted in a humusy soil mixture. Thus we save ourselves the trouble of lifting a large plant each year yet safeguard its future. Sun, moisture, humidity, liquid fertilizer may some day in January bring forth a green bud which, if we keep our fingers crossed, reveals the lovely blossom.

Had we no other climbing plants, the passion vine would entwine itself around the wires that outline the window frame. But competition for this service is still another chapter.

32. Vines That Take to Water

A NUMBER of the prettiest vines take as naturally to water as ducklings to a sunny pond. If you are just venturing into this hobby of house plants, growing vines in water is an encouraging way to begin. We have always been enthusiastic about this method, first, because it affords opportunity to use our choicest vases and then, because cultural experience has indicated that water-filled vases are extremely valuable humidifiers when placed among house plants.

English ivy roots readily in water if lengths of it are cut in August when the sap is high and the plants are still enthusiastic about beginning a new life in a different environment which in this case is our shaded porch. Too often indoor gardeners fail with ivy cuttings because they wait until the weather is cold and the plants going dormant before they remember about their indoor bouquets. Then they rush out on a frosty October morning, cut sprays and spend a lot of time arranging them only to see them going into a wilting decline a few days later in the heat of the house.

We used to get caught this way too, but now we mark August twentieth as Ivy Day on our calendars. With a sharp knife we repair to the garden that day and cut long and short sections — twelve-inch pieces are particularly reliable — from the ivy climbing up our old apple tree. We place the cuttings loosely — to allow free air circulation — in a pail of water on the shaded porch for a month. Extra water is added every few days and no leaves permitted to rest below the water line because they deteriorate there and foul the water.

It is a good plan we find to cut more sprays than we actually need because some fail to root. Often some of the slow pieces begin growing, however, if the ends are snipped again after about ten days. Vases are arranged indoors in mid-September and for the first weeks plenty of fresh air is admitted and the ivy sprays held daily under a splashy faucet. The full force of the cold water on the leaves seems to be just what the doctor ordered and gets the bouquets off to a beautiful shining start.

In case all this seems too much trouble, you can, of course, buy potted ivy from the florist and wash the soil off its nice root system in order to turn it into a vase plant. Once established, ivy indoors will grow in sun or shade but not in the dark as many fondly hope who place it on dim mantel ends.

After a winter's sojourn with you, it will enjoy a summer on the shaded porch. A pretty bracket tacked to pillar or house wall will display it just as effectively as your indoor vases. And incidentally as soon as it is rooted a plant tablet dropped monthly into each vase will prove a nutritionally super meal.

Other vines that do well in water are climbing nasturtiums, philodendron, tradescantia and coleus (if you can keep this last free of mealy bug). The nasturtiums will not be permanent residents but if you cut healthful long sprays (give a Black Leaf 40 cleanup, if a single aphid is visible) in late September and after placing in water add a bit of liquid fertilizer each week you may be delighted to find that from October on into March there is a sweet procession of scarlet, yellow and orange blooms. It only seems to take about six or seven days after cutting for roots to begin to form. Of course, such a charmer rates a sunny spot, a weekly syringing and the frequent addition of water.

Philodendron and the other trailers in bowls and vases lead in our house a peripatetic life. Sometimes jars of them adorn our deep living-room window sills. Sometimes the same pieces become arrangements when with clusters of scarlet geranium or delicate sprays of primrose or begonia they adorn the dining table for a party. Philodendron roots even more readily than ivy in water and in full sun or light grows at a nice fast clip. It is well worth buying several rooted plants and transforming them into bouquets for any room in the house.

This vine also needs a weekly faucet bath, a monthly meal and quantities of fresh water to keep it happy. An attractive display trick for it is to fill a row of choice tea cups with pebbles and tuck philodendron lengths into their anchoring depths. In our geranium picture you can see how we did this at either end of the first short glass shelf. Here the philodendron soon rooted and sent out new growth. By spring it had developed most exuberantly.

33. The Indispensable Vines

THE undercurrent to our theme of house plants has been vines. Without them the window garden loses that graciousness, which springs from a living green frame around the plant picture. Even those who are not rabid house plant collectors succumb to a vine somewhere about the house. It may be only a length of ivy twined in a bowl on the dining table or pots of sad philodendron on the mantelpiece. Nevertheless they are there — mute testimony to the hardiness and indispensability of vines.

We were quite amazed one winter's day to count up eighteen different vines, flourishing about the house.

They ranged from the plumbago blooming delicately at the south window to *Cissus antarctica* on the mantelpiece, *Cissus striata* on a bracket in the bathroom and lengths of *Vinca minor* and bits of tradescantia in colored glassware temporarily brightening the window. So aptly did each vine suit its location that no one of them dominated a room.

Ivy, of course, is the vine which most people want to grow. We are partial to the small-leaved Pittsburgh type and use four-inch pots of it to soften the edge of the radiator tray in the window garden. If we collected ivies we could write a whole chapter about them. Since we never have, we can only recommend Pittsburgh or one of the other small-leaved varieties as sturdiest for average house conditions. At that they will be short-lived unless they are kept out of full sunlight and grown humid and in a reasonably cool place. Moderate daily watering and a vigorous top washing at least once every week to ward off red spider are vital.

Most enduring of all vines is *Cissus antarctica* or kangaroo. Its clean saw-edged leaves are a little large to frame a window garden but in tolerance and longevity it is a bracket plant without equal. Neither bugs, diseases, heat nor neglect disturb the even tenor of its growth. Six years is the record set by one of our plants at a west window. When stems grow too long, they are clipped off and rooted in water for new plants and on the old one new side shoots appear.

The finely cut, smaller leaves of *Cissus striata* are daintier but the plants themselves are more delicate and susceptible to the devastating red spider. It's a delightful little vine for a cool and light situation.

Ideal for framing the window garden and nearly as thrifty as kangaroo vine are grape ivy and philodendron. Actually, grape ivy is also a Cissus but its foliage has the dark glossiness of English ivy with downy leaf buds and short reddish tendrils to enhance its decorativeness.

St. Louis ivy or *Philodendron cordatum* is the old standby for dim places within a room and all other thankless house plant jobs. Its only drawback is the tendency to become stringy with age as the space between the heart-shaped leaves gets longer and longer. The cure is pinching off the stems at a good-looking point and putting the detached pieces in water to root.

One year our florist had a spotted philodendron which in all other respects duplicated the standard green variety. It was highly effective. We also like *Philodendron dubiae* with larger deeply lobed leaves that remind us of the foliage of the white oak tree. This, too, is a pace setter for long life and good health. It lives equally well in water or soil and prefers to grow upward rather than down. Nephthytis with its arrow-shaped leaves also likes to grow this way and is a stunning specimen plant.

Third of our thrifty vines is Pothos, although it grows more slowly and is a bit heavy textured to make a good climber for the window. It is as handsome a vine as there is, particularly the variety Wilcoxi which has green leaves streaked with white or cream. Pothos prefers light and grows steadily if not too rapidly throughout the years.

All foliage vines are easy plants. With the possible exception of English ivy, they will grow under the most average conditions. None of them need sun yet the texture of most of them is tough enough to stand whatever they receive at the side of a south window. They will be happier, of course, and less bleached in color in an east or west window or somewhere within a room where they may dwell in light only. Neither are most vines particular as to temperature or humidity, although fresh air is conducive to good health and good looks.

The upkeep of vines follows a simple pattern with the exception, perhaps, of the true ivies. They like moderate watering daily or, depending on the situation, may be satisfied with it every other day. Needless to say, a weekly syringing is highly advisable. This keeps foliage clean, dust free and healthy and, of course, affords an opportunity to nip insect attacks before they obtain a foothold.

Taken by and large, vines are diverse in their habit of growth and in their appearance and will perform a multitude of different services. Between the two media of water and soil, they may be accommodated wherever they fit into the decorative scheme of our homes.

Vines

Flowering

Black-eyed Susan *(Thunbergia alata)*   South

Confederate Jasmine (*Trachelo-
  spermum jasminoides*)   East, West, South
Jasmine (*Jasminum grandiflo-
  rum*)   South, East
Morning Glory   South
Passion Vine (*Passiflora caerulea*) South
Plumbago capensis   South
Tradescantia   East, West, South
Wax Plant (*Hoya carnosa*)   South, East

Foliage

  Cissus antarctica   East, West, North
  Cissus striata   East, West
  Coleus   South, East, West
  Grape Ivy   East, West
  Ivy   West, North
  Nephthytis   East, West, North
  Philodendron   East, West, North
  Pothos aureus   East, West, North
  Sweet Potato   East
  Tradescantia   West
  Vinca minor   South, East
  Zebrina pendulosa   East, West

Light Only

  Cissus antarctica
  Ivy
  Nephthytis
  Philodendron
  Pothos
  Zebrina

Water

Cissus antarctica
Coleus
Ivy
Passion Vine
Nephthytis
Periwinkle, Myrtle (Vinca minor)
Philodendron
    P. cordatum
    P. dubiae
Pothos aureus
Tradescantia
Zebrina pendulosa

Portfolio

OF

HOUSE PLANTS USED DECORATIVELY

THEIR ARRANGEMENT
IN WINDOW GARDENS

AND AS

ORNAMENTAL OCCASIONAL PLANTS
SINGLY AND IN GROUPS

SEE PAGE 220 FOR LIST OF PLANTS
APPEARING IN PHOTOGRAPH PORTFOLIO

Forecast of Spring. Glistening white wax begonias and fairy primroses have their serenity enlivened by china kittens collected all over the world.

A Mantel Study in Enduring Green. The sturdy kangaroo vine
thrives in place while the dish garden and copper tray are moved
to a bright window for a few hours each morning.

Welcome the Guest. The cyclamen on a pebble filled saucer with a protective circle of oil cloth or wax paper beneath, ivy and nar-cissus are moved to the hall only on below forty degree nights.

Thanksgiving in Average Window fitted with glass shelves to hold a number of permanent plants and flanked with gift chrysanthemums for the occasion.

Christmas brings a change of accessories and gift plants. The narcissus have come into bloom, poinsettias have replaced the chrysanthemums and kalanchoes entered the picture.

Valentine's Day ushers in nostalgic china figures and gay cyclamen but the basic green frame remains, and kalanchoe and African violets still flower.

Winter Sunshine, true or false, appears with pots of florists' daffodils while home grown callas play an important role. Roman hyacinths are also starting to flower.

Orchid at Home. Under a Victorian glass dome this beauteous green orchid thinks it is in a greenhouse. The slatted blind protects it from full sun.

Bookcase ending. Here the fascinating ardisia holds its fruit until June, and the pittosporum and variegated anthericum afford pleasing foliage contrast.

Bright Medley in an Apartment Window. A sunny window accommodates a hobby collection of flowering and foliage plants always in the best of condition.

Gay Fruit for Winter. A tier table becomes a plant stand for orange
tree and cherries softened with vines and ferns with a tile beneath
each pot to protect the polished surface.

Conversation Piece for Mealtime. In the dining room, a recessed window holds feathery ferns and vines highlighted with seasonal flowers. Here pink poinsettias are framed by golden draperies.

Variety in Vines. In a Pennsylvania Dutch setting, contrasting leaf patterns of plants growing in soil and in water make interesting silhouettes. Even Freckles finds this an appealing spot.

Cacti and Succulents. A suspended double shelf contains green growing things which entertain the busy person who can supply only moderately good care and conditions.

Behind the Scenes. A small closet containing (below) all the para-
phernalia for house plant care, even a place to spray, and (above) a
number of accessories for altering the window garden.

CHAPTER IX

MULTIPLICATION OF HOUSE PLANTS

THE neighborly habit of exchanging slips of favorite plants dates back to Colonial times. Even in those early days women realized that one of the easiest ways of creating a sense of home in a strange place was to grow there familiar and dearly loved plants. So they treasured the bit of geranium or patience plant as much as they enjoyed the cup of tea which went with the gift, and then with careful hand grew the small green branch to flowering maturity.

Today we may be more learned about the various means of propagating our house plants but slips, or as we term them, cuttings, are still an easy means of multiplication. First there are the simple stem cuttings which quickly form roots in a proper medium. This is usually clean sharp sand but geraniums, wax begonias, coleus, tradescantia and ivy will even develop into complete plants in water.

Generally speaking, cuttings need moisture, a moderate even temperature and an atmosphere not too dry.

Some plants, however, are so easy to propagate, that practically all you need is the little piece of fresh green growth. Just now, for example, we have a nice little crop of young geraniums coming along in the soil at the edges of the big plants. A month ago we inserted a number of broken off pieces an inch deep. They are rooted now and ready for transplanting.

A friend who manages a lot of plants on very little time, avoids shifting cuttings through several pot sizes by filling at the outset three-inch pots with the average house plant mixture but with a little ball of clean sand in the center. Into this sand she inserts her cuttings. They root readily there and as the developing plants need more nutrition, they find it by growing beyond the confines of the lump of sand.

Another easy method of dealing with cuttings is to transform a fish aquarium into a greenhouse and grow them there. In the bottom of the bowl spread an inch of drainage material — small stones or coarse gravel. Then spread two inches of sand or light garden soil. Moisten this thoroughly so that it is damp but not soggy. Insert cuttings of your favorites and cover the top with a pane of glass. Set the bowl in a light not sunny place and if water collects on the glass, lift and wipe it. Extra watering is usually not necessary. As the plants form roots, they are lifted and potted separately in average soil.

Our own favorite multiplication device (see drawing, page 179) is an eight-inch bulb pan. In the center of this is placed a corked three-inch flower pot filled with water. The space between pot and pan is firmly packed with

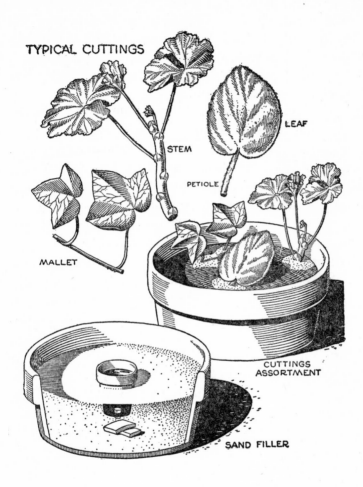

TYPICAL CUTTINGS

LEAF

STEM

PETIOLE

MALLET

CUTTINGS
ASSORTMENT

SAND FILLER

sand. Various kinds of cuttings are inserted in the sand, geranium, begonia, ivy, poinsettia, cactus, etc. All are kept evenly moist by water seeping through the walls of the center pot into the sand. More water is added as the supply goes down. You can use this pot-in-pan system either indoors in a light place or outside on the shaded porch or under an arbor.

Suppose, for example, that you want a new crop of geraniums or wax begonias for next winter. In June when you transfer the house plants to summer quarters, take a number of cuttings and insert them immediately in the prepared pan. Select pieces of young growth, firm but not woody. Discard that which is either sappy or hard. With geraniums, a stem is in proper condition to make a good cutting if, when bent, it snaps but does not break through entirely, a few of the fibres holding.

Make the cuts sharply, on the slant, and only just below a node or point of growth which you can feel as a little bump along the stem. Let each piece be three or four inches long and contain at least two nodes and three internodes or spaces between. Avoid bruising. Remove the lower leaves and any little wings on the stems. Cut off flower buds and also any very large top leaves. If too much top growth exists, cuttings wilt and die because there is no root system to supply moisture. There must be a few leaves, however, since these are the food manufacturing centers. Finally, insert the cuttings so that at least two nodes are covered.

It takes two to three weeks, varying with the kind of plant, for stem cuttings to form roots. A slight tug — but no fair for at least a week — will indicate if they are rooted and ready to be planted in their own pots of soil.

Leaves of certain plants can also be encouraged to develop roots. The outstanding example is the African violet. Insert a firm, thrifty leaf the length of its own leaf stem or petiole in either sand or water. Small, fleshy leaves of the jade plant or crassula also root easily when partially buried in sand.

The foliage of many other house plants can be so cut as to reproduce in an interesting fashion. English ivy soon forms thrifty new plants if a piece of stem plus a single leaf is planted in sand. This is called a mallet cutting (see page 179). And, if there is anyone anywhere who ever wants more sansevierias or snake plants, all that is necessary is to remove one long vigorous leaf, cut it into approximately two-inch sections and place these in a pot of sand with the cut edge, which was nearest the root, set downward.

Large-leaved begonias are fascinating to play with. Choose a mature leaf and sever it with a half-inch stub of stem. Then slash through the main veins for about an inch and lay the leaf on the surface of the sand, weighting it in close contact with a few pebbles. Or if the begonia leaf is a very large one, snip it into triangles and slide the pointed ends well into the sand. In either case roots form and a cluster of new leaves appears at the leaf cuts or the triangle's point.

All these cuttings are a comparatively simple matter, while raising house plants from seed is often a long and tedious process. It requires time to have them develop into mature plants and vigilance while they are doing so. Many kinds including the African violet, geranium, cyclamen and asparagus fern can be managed without benefit of greenhouse. But the average indoor gardener will be preoccupied with established plants and hoard her seed efforts for the more easily grown ones or those hard to procure except at the seed stage.

Primroses, flowering maple, special varieties of sem-perflorens begonia, and Christmas cherries we think are worth while in order to obtain a generous display of the finer varieties for decorative massing. Maturing plants will be ready for winter bloom if the seed is sown the previous year between January and May.

In case you are familiar with vegetables you will be pleased to hear that the procedure is just as simple as that for starting tomatoes from seed indoors. Briefly, the seeds are sown in pots of sandy soil. Some house plant seed is so small that it is not covered at all but scattered on the soil surface and then protected by a piece of glass resting on the rim of the pot. Warmth and even moisture are thus assured. When seedlings appear, the pot is moved from dimness to light which is required by the developing plants.

Seedlings will need to be transplanted to prevent loss from damping off and to allow room for normal growth. Several shiftings are then advisable between the two leaf stage and the full-fledged plants of the window garden.

If there is time, facilities and patience, any true house plants of which seed can be obtained may be attempted.

It is comforting to realize, however, that even if you are a novice you are bound to have success from some of the garden plants such as the morning glory and black-eyed Susan vine. These you can count on for pleasure in return for the sowing of a single packet of seeds.

CHAPTER X

REST AND VACATION FOR
HOUSE PLANTS

PLANTS are not always in a state of growth even though they do appear fresh and green. All of them have weary off seasons, not always so apparent as in the poinsettia and cyclamen which frankly discard their leaves at some time in the year and so announce: "We are going to sleep." With most other indoor plants it is quite a trick to recognize the difference between a resting plant and a starved plant.

When all the cultural factors are good and there are no signs of insect or disease and yet a plant unfurls no leaf nor sets a single bud, the obvious conclusion should be that it's not stubborn nor lazy but tired. It wants an undisturbed nap at such a point in its life cycle, and neither the stimulation of food nor repotting will be good for it. What is really needed is less light, less heat and less water. In other words, the quiet life. During such semi- or completely dormant weeks the amaryllis and cyclamen are best in a dark retreat while many foliage plants simply stand where they are. Only close

observation of the individual subjects you grow will re-
veal this condition of rest.

Usually ferns and palms are quiescent along with
many other window garden favorites in early winter. At
the turn of the year, they seem to wake up. New fronds
appear. The same is true of vines such as the philodendron which may be indifferent about progress until
January but then by March get going like mad. Geraniums rest at your convenience, but rest they will, either
in winter or summer, for they refuse to bloom the entire
year. This is natural enough considering the hard work
they are capable of in either six months' stretch. Except
for the Thanksgiving and Christmas cacti, many plants
of this type are also fairly dormant during the early
cold months preferring to set flowers in spring and to
produce then, according to their kind, new bumps or
strands of growth.

In May or early June, if valuable and permanent house
plants are to preserve their looks for another year they
need a resuscitation period out of doors. Here under
nature's ideal growing conditions most of them are able
to recover from the frustrations of house life and to store
up a reserve of health for the next winter ahead.

Before they go on vacation, however, an unprejudiced
inventory is not amiss. Have these plants future decorative possibilities is a question well worth an unsenti-
mental answer. Besides we find after several years that
we tire of certain rather static appearing foliage subjects
and want other varieties for background or accent.

Therefore about once in three years there is terrific

mortality, come spring, in our window garden, especially when we start considering every house plant on the basis of size. We refuse, in fact, to be saddled with a hoard of five-inch subjects which a few years before at the three-inch stage were perfect for our decorative purposes. If these are in health we pass them on to organizations, often school or church, ' where their fresh greenness will give pleasure and their size be an asset, not a liability.

Leggy dracaenas and sprawling begonias, plain-jane crassulas or defeated ferns, however, are simply discarded via ashcan. So too do we deal with such "florists' annuals" as the cinerarias, calceolarias and primroses which have no second season possibilities. As for the bulbs, forced tender paperwhite narcissus are permitted a painless passing. Other bulbs, their foliage having matured, are saved for future planting. The hardy Dutch bulbs — tulips, daffodils and hyacinths — are planted in some sunny and permanent outdoor garden location in the fall while lachenalia and freesia and their ilk are stored to be repotted for next winter's indoor display.

Good cutting material is now available from geraniums and wax begonias which have been flowering all winter. The cuttings will be nice small plants by autumn and after this pruning and a summer's incubation, the old ones may even have possibilities for next winter's window garden.

The majority of house plants do have a future if their summer accommodations have been chosen to help restore the vigor lost under the forced and often trying conditions of winter quarters. We wouldn't think of discarding our vines and small foliage plants or the holly fern. And plumbago, sweet olive, azaleas, poinsettias and African violets will, if properly cared for, live to pay dividends.

Thus is indicated another day's work that is inescapable. Some pleasant morning when frosts no longer threaten, all of the plants are taken out to the grape arbor. One by one we settle their fate, and they are top-dressed or repotted or left severely alone as their appearance dictates.

Of the plants we are keeping, some such as African violet will return to the safety of the porch. (We may even decide to take a few, such as the tree-like pittosporum or leafy spathiphyllum, back indoors to relieve the bareness of the window garden.) Vines will adorn the window box or porch bracket while other plants are plunged in the garden. Wherever they go outside of four walls, they are placed near enough for occasional watering and inspection and out of prevailing winds. Experience has taught us to leave the plants in their pots, for given the freedom of a garden bed roots will roam so widely that the September moving is slowed and the plants' growth checked by the root pruning which is unavoidable in repotting.

The spot chosen for our plants outdoors always offers varying amounts of shade so that the sun-loving geranium will feel as much at home as the shade-loving fern. A small, spreading tree such as a red maple or a tall open one, an apple or elm, takes care of them all. Ferns and most foliage plants go where shade is deepest. The next circle under the more open branches, yet with some shade, is built up of such flowering plants as azaleas and gardenias, begonias and sweet olive and the fruit plants.

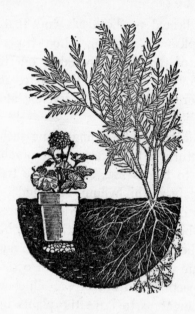

Just inside the outer rim of the branches but not under their worst drip go poinsettia, young geraniums, and semperflorens begonias.

The quickest way to settle all these individuals is to dig a bed deep enough to hold the largest pot above a three-inch layer of cinders, stone or any rough material that will prove too difficult a tunneling job for worms. Over this foundation the plants are placed according to their light needs. Then the bed is filled not quite to the rim of the pots with a light soil containing water-holding peatmoss or humus. Of course you may do this plunging job less scientifically but more quickly by loosening soil for each plant, dropping some drainage material in the bottom of the hole, and then firming the pot in place.

It should not be a case of out of sight, out of mind for house plants in summer. Occasionally each plant is turned round so that roots which have worked through the drainage hole will not anchor it. Summer rainfall cannot be depended on for adequate moisture, so periodic watering will be necessary. These attentions afford an opportunity to watch for any insect appearances. Such should be scotched by hosing or spraying as promptly as in winter. Then, too, pinching a leaf tip here or pruning an exuberant side branch there will encourage shapely growth for potential winter beauties.

CHAPTER XI

CHURCH PLANTS HAVE
FEELINGS TOO

LATELY when we come home from church on Sunday we are in a dither — the preaching is so lively, the plants so dead. To people as garden-minded as we are there is something painfully distracting about an exalted sermon rising from the midst of deteriorating plants. We try to concentrate but in our minds it invariably happens that the text gets mixed up with what we would do with those palms, ferns and ivies if it were up to us to guarantee their looks and health from Sunday to Sunday.

Many churches, of course, wisely rent their green plants. The florist carefully brings them in on Saturday and removes them to his refreshing greenhouse and knowing ministrations on Monday. Hence they always appear in the pink. Our religious sect, however, seems to hold little truck with beauty. We place cleanliness next to godliness and try to be good at both high living and high thinking. But by the look of things, the contribution of beauty to the spirit is not universally respected. So along with many other churches, we save the florist's fees and leave the altar decorations to an only moderately interested committee. Hence the brittle palms, the arid ivies and the yellowing ferns of our complaint.

Yet all three of these plant groups are fairly tolerant of medium conditions. If after Sunday services they could be moved (carefully protected, if necessary, from chilling by newspaper wrapping) to a moderately sunny window in the Chapter House where the temperature did not drop below 55° F. at night, nor soar above 70 in the daytime, and where some interested custodian would regard our five-point good looks program, they would, come Sunday, be fit for their important decorative rôle of altar adornment.

Since ferns and ivies (page 94 and page 172) have already been discussed, we will here only go into the important matter of palms. Because of their dignified form and excellent size in maturity they are the finest of church plants. They do require plenty of room, however, since the careless brushing of passers-by readily breaks or bruises foliage and so destroys the symmetrical growth which is so essential a part of the beauty of each well-grown specimen.

Two of the finest varieties are the royal palms — the erect *Kentia belmoreana* and the spreading *K. forsteriana*, both of which are obligingly slow growing and tolerant of our human ways. These grow from a single central stem. Belmoreana is the more graceful of the two.

Other kinds to be considered when the church palms

are being purchased, are the cone palm, *Areca lutescens*, a faster growing cluster type with golden stems, and the Chinese fan palm, *Phoenix roebelini*, a broad, dwarf strong-growing variety. For placement in the foreground of a group the small and elegant cocoanut palm, *Cocos weddeliana*, is pleasing.

Palms are slow to show neglect but equally slow to recover from it. Usually if they have gone into a decline they can be brought to health again only after a year of greenhouse conditions. In that case new plants are often the cheapest way out for the committee. When they are healthy and growing properly palms will put out usually in spring or summer several new fans a year, each larger than the one which preceded it. If it is smaller, lighter in color and imperfect, opening out before it is completely formed, overwatering is indicated, and it is more than likely that the plant has been allowed to stand in stagnant water.

This is the worst possible condition but often occurs when palms are kept in jardinieres which are not scrubbed frequently on the inside and emptied regularly after plants are watered. A layer of stones or a block of wood placed in the jardiniere so that the palm always rests above a possible watering residue is an excellent safety measure — but no substitute for a weekly inside scrubbing.

Palms are best grown in relatively small pots for their size. An areca, for example, which is four feet tall with six to seven leaves is adequately accommodated by a seven-inch pot. Usually repotting every other year suffices and then the shift is only to the next size pot. Palms are fed in spring and summer and at all times kept free from dust. Wiping or sponging the leaves frequently with a clean damp cloth is refreshing, where spraying is inconvenient. At the same time any invasion of scale or mealy bug may be detected and removed (page 49) before they have multiplied to the extent of harming the palm's appearance.

Watering must be thorough enough to reach the deepest portions of the roots. Since these are often heavily coiled this plant is benefited by being placed weekly in a pail of water until it has drawn up sufficient moisture to make the surface soil damp. In-between watering may also be necessary once or twice a week. If such watering is constant but light and the lower roots suffer from continuous drought, the plant will gradually turn a sickly yellow. When leaves turn brown it is usually the result of a drought or chill from a sudden change in temperature.

Twice a year, many churches add flowering plants to the existing greenery. Usually these are poinsettias for Christmas and hydrangeas at Easter. The busy florist cannot bring them in only an hour before service — he must do it the day before. And though he will give them a final watering before he leaves, these two handsome flowering plants need quantities of moisture if their heads are not to droop before the assembled congregation. It should be someone's duty to see that these plants are watered again late on Saturday, and early Sunday morning; and to make certain also that no nearby windows are left open so that a draught will strike the blooms. The itinerant plants, alas, are more touchy than the perennial palm.

Whatever the plants and however many Sundays they appear in churches, they must be regarded as growing things. They cannot be treated like furniture which is moved in and out of the church by just anybody. They need a modicum of intelligent care and always careful handling if they are to fill their important rôle of decoration and so contribute rather than detract from the service of which they can so definitely be a part.

CALENDAR OF CHORES

JANUARY

Amaryllis. Is the flower stalk appearing on your *new* plant? If so, move it gradually to light and sun and heat (not above 70° F., please) and increase the water supply as need is indicated. Every other week, apply one-half cup liquid manure. Examine your *older* stored amaryllis for signs of life. Then renew top layer of soil and water. Keep cool and dim until stalk is about three inches high.

Araucaria. The development of a new circle of leaves is a sign to begin feeding this active growing plant.

Azalea. Place your Christmas present away from full

195

sunlight until the flowers have faded. Then give it a bright spot. The cool side, that is 60° F. or less and much water, even twice daily, are other needs.

Broad-leaved Foliage Plants. When you recover from the holidays, give your rubber plants, dracaenas, etc., a big treat. Go over all the leaf surfaces, above and below, with a soft cloth dipped in mild soap suds.

Bulbs. If you have tulips, hyacinths, etc., in a pit outdoors, bring them in now to a cold light window.

Cactus. This is the best time to repot since plants have just finished resting. Once in two or three years is frequent enough.

Christmas Cactus. Decrease watering after flowering stops. If no flowers yet, keep in full sun but avoid overwatering. Every third day usually suffices.

Cyclamen. Take care that there is always water in the saucer under this plant.

Daffodils. Plant a few good forcing varieties like Conspicuus and White Lady in pebbles and water late this month.

Funkia. Bring the potted funkia into a warm room and water it freely to stimulate leaf and flower production. Both are pretty.

Geraniums. Move rested plants back to sun and warmth (up to 65° F.). As growth develops, water more freely and apply liquid fertilizer on a fortnightly schedule.

Hyacinths, Dutch, in glasses. Bring to heat and warmth (after ten to twelve rooting weeks) for forcing late this month.

Hydrangea. Transfer to a sunny window, gradually increase amount of watering. Resume feeding schedule.

Roses. The miniatures, Tom Thumb and Pixie, will gladly blossom ahead of their June schedule if you will move them now to a 65° F. location in full sun. Shower tops weekly by way of encouragement.

Watch out for pests this month and next. After so many weeks of less-humid-than-they-like air, some plants will be easy prey. Reread the five-point program to check up on basic care.

FEBRUARY

African Violet. Keep watch these cold days of roaring furnaces that air is not stuffy or dry. Syringe plants with warm water, keep from sun till dry.

Amaryllis. Cut away the faded flowering stem if your new plant has bloomed. Continue to tend it in the window. Feeding goes on until late in August. Your older plant may soon be ready to emerge from the cellar. First replace top inch or so of soil with a fresh mixture plus one teaspoon of bone meal.

Asparagus Fern. Beware of too much heat or sun which causes yellowing of foliage.

Bleeding Hearts. Dig a clump of this from the garden any mild day now that you can sink a spade into the earth. Spiraea, candytuft and primroses are other possibilities. Pot these and urge them with sunshine, water and warmth to bloom soon for you.

Bouvardia. Take cuttings now for next year's plants. Discard those which have ceased flowering.

Cactus. Keep in a warm sunny window this month and into summer. Brush tops occasionally to remove dust and water twice a week, not more, maybe less if specimens are large.

Camellias. As you see flower buds forming, increase the water supply.

Christmas Cherry. Sow a pot of seed, collected from the dried pulp of last year's gift plant.

Cyclamen. Pull out faded flowers and leaves sharply from the base of the plant.

Daffodils. If these have had two weeks of dark, cool pebble and water growing, provide a new residence in some cool and sunny window.

Easter Lilies. Transfer these now to a warmer location

(about 68° F.) and permit full sunlight. Feed with liquid manure every other week.

Ferns. Remove those root runners which creep out from the fern base. They use up energy for no good purpose.

Kalanchoe. Watch out for mealy bug any time now.

Marguerites. Discover these at the florist this month and brighten up your window garden with their gay yellow blooms. Submerge the pots in water for one hour out of every twenty-four.

Marica. This is one not to snip. Let flowers fade into ensuing small new plants.

Morning Glories. Sow seeds, preferably of Heavenly Blue, six to a five-inch pot. Thin later to three and you should have your first rewarding bloom in ten weeks time.

Orange and Lemon Trees. Place in quarters as warm as 65° F. As spring gets nearer they are losing their interest in fruits and thinking about blossoms again.

Pandanus. Cut off below soil level those little green youngsters thrusting up beside the parent. Separately potted, they will soon grow into fine tall plants.

Poinsettia. Leaves turning yellow now indicate a need for sleep. Slow up water supply and store plant in a cool (60° F.) dry place until spring. (The unheated guest room is a possibility!)

Strelitzia. Bring it back to warmth after its rest and when new growth appears, begin the fortnightly feeding schedule. Keep this up until December.

There are enchanting primroses in the shops this month to freshen up the window garden picture. Why not send yourself a Valentine of three lacy white primroses or select an enchanting cloud of misty lavender ones? They will stay pretty for weeks and in their blooming condition require only light not sun. So for a green window of foliage and vine plants, they are ideal accents.

MARCH

African Violet. Plants purchased in October may now need division if flowering has ceased and the crown seems leaf jammed. Remember this one needs *overpotting* with plenty of leafmold. Insert for a bright future one or two of those big leaves its stem length in a tiny pot of sandy soil.

Christmas Cherry. Dry the fruits when they fall. Extract the seeds and sow for a new crop. Cut back each branch to two eyes. Move the plant to a 40° F. light spot.

Gardenia. Be very certain soil never really dries out. A just moist condition is essential if those fat slow buds are to open properly.

Geraniums. Cut back any overlong shoots and turn the plants at the window to keep them stocky and shapely. If growth is lush and long and leaves are small, plants are probably being grown too warm.

Hydrangeas. Take cuttings.

Narcissus. If any paperwhites remain, better plant at once. From rooting to blooming will take less than three weeks now.

Orange and Lemon Trees. Give some liquid manure as new growth appears this month.

Palms. Begin liquid manure feedings now as new growth develops. Continue through the summer.

Primroses. For a riot of color next January, sow seed now of *Primula obconica*, the Top Primrose, or *P. malacoides*, the dainty baby type. One kind and one color is best for a season.

Those brown twigs on the forsythia bushes in the garden will in a week or two turn goldenrod yellow at your window. Just cut a few and place them in a deep vase of water in the sun where they will lighten up the whole house plant picture.

APRIL

Cactus. Cut off sharply small pieces of new green growth this month or next. Dry off. Then insert one-half inch deep in small pots of sandy soil.

Camellia. Allow more warmth to stimulate growth as flowering wanes.

Christmas Cherry. When new top growth appears late this month, move to a sunny 50 to 60° F. spot and water more freely.

Cyclamen. No longer maintain a constant inch of water in the pot saucer but give less and less until in a few weeks the top of the plant is dry. Remove this spent growth and dust the exposed part of the corm with powdered sulphur. Place the plant on its side in a cool dark room. Moisten soil about once in two weeks.

Hydrangea. Water if necessary twice daily. This plant has a colossal thirst when it starts growing.

Primrose. Sow seeds of the Chinese type, *P. sinensis.*

On warm pleasant afternoons, open the windows to give your plants a foretaste of summer. Watch out for chills though and beware the refreshing shower outside. Your house-bound plants are tender. Slat the blind at times or draw the glass curtain across if sunshine is causing any wilting of foliage.

MAY

Abutilon. Sow seeds this month for flowering plants by autumn.

African Violet. The eastern sun is getting too hot so better move to north window or draw thin curtain.

Azalea. Repot the tender ones in acid soil for future window beauty. Feed regularly each month with liquid manure. Find a permanent open shady spot for hardy varieties (remember the large flowering kinds are the tender ones).

Bulbs. Store the hardy ones with matured foliage in their pots in a cool, airy place until fall.

Christmas Cactus. Shift to a little larger pot only if absolutely necessary.

Coleus. For next year's bright plants, take cuttings now and root in sand or water.

Cyclamen. Late this month take the Cyclamen outside and lay the pot on its side by a house wall or under a grape arbor. Water occasionally.

Gardenia. After you have had it a month, give it fortnightly liquid manure doses. Continue until September.

Geraniums. Take cuttings later this month or early next for winter flowering plants.

Marica. Cut off and pot the new little plants appearing on the tips of the leaves just where flowers once opened.

Poinsettia. It awaits rediscovery. Prune to six inches. Repot, water and return to sun and heat. Make cuttings of the new growth which soon will appear.

Strawberry Begonia. Detach now those fascinating small plants hanging by threads from the big one. Separately potted, they will make rapid growth.

Wax Plant. After the starry clusters of bloom fade, cherish the flower stems. These are the source of next year's blossoms.

Late in the month when settled warmth outdoors is

certain, take a morning for repotting and summer quartering. Decide what is to be plunged and what for the porch. Be ruthless about misfits and sickly specimens. Get rid of everything without a future for you.

JUNE

Calla, white. Insist on a nap starting this month and continuing for three. Less water and laying the calla on its side makes the plant sleepy.

Geraniums. Hold on to the large, older plants only if you will have room next winter for this size. Trim each branch back five or six inches and shift on to next size pots. Plunge in a fairly sunny garden spot.

Hydrangea. Cut back hard, each stem to two sets of buds. Then repot if necessary in a one size larger container or on large tubbed specimens replace upper few inches of soil.

Get firmly in mind a watering and top syringing schedule for your now less interesting house plants. Note that evaporation is much higher for porch than for window plants and that summer rainfall is far from adequate for the plunged specimens.

JULY

Calla, yellow. Make it rest now by gradually reducing water and laying plant on its side in a cool shady place.

Christmas Cherry. Begin fortnightly feedings and continue until fruits show color.

Gardenia. Be strong minded and pinch off all summer buds. It's winter bloom you really crave.

Geraniums. Order your fall and winter flowering material from the florist *early* this month. He needs time to get them started. Keep buds pinched off older plants you are holding over. Turn and trim plants frequently to keep stocky and shapely.

Orange and Lemon Trees. While they prepare next year's crop, a bi-monthly feeding will strengthen them.

Don't forget your house plants even if the summer heat and humidity have you practically glued to a porch rocker. Frequent watering and occasional pest cleaning are still the order of the day.

AUGUST

Amaryllis. Cease its feeding at end of this month.

Black-Eyed Susan Vine. Sow seeds now of this *Thunbergia alata*, five to a three-inch pot. Thin if necessary to three plants. You will be rewarded with early winter flowers

Calla, white. Pot first bulbs for November bloom. Select six-inch pots for big varieties, four-inch for small. Moisten and set in a dim cool place. Water sparingly until top growth commences.

Cyclamen. Examine for signs of new growth. When these appear, repot corm with as much adhering earth as possible in fresh soil to which a little tobacco dust and some rotted cow manure, if this is available, has been added (three tablespoons to a five-inch pot). Set corm high, upper half protruding and tip on a line with pot rim. Water and place again, but right side up, under arbor or on a sheltered porch.

Hydrangea. Begin bi-monthly liquid manure feedings for this plant and remember about need for frequent watering.

Ivy, English. Take bouquet cuttings now (don't wait till cold autumn nights harden the tissue) and root them in a pail of water set on the porch. Cut off all below-the-water-line foliage.

Geraniums. May and June cuttings are now ready for separate potting in three-inch pots of a quite firm soil mixture.

Plumbago capensis. Toward the end of this month start thinning out the tops a little and cutting them back a few inches preparatory to bringing the plants indoors. You will notice that growth during summer has been amazing.

Poinsettia. Prune according to future use. Back to two inches for table plants. Less than one-third off for the window garden subjects.

Consider now next winter's house plants. There is ordering and potting of bulbs to be done and plans for next winter's succession of color and bloom to be arranged. Repaint clay pots for fall use, first removing old paint with sandpaper. Three coats will delay blistering.

SEPTEMBER

Annuals. From the garden lift and pot small thrifty plants of snapdragon, marigolds, etc., suitable for the window. Trim these back a little and set on the porch steps in the sun (after a two-day shady retreat immediately following the potting) while they acclimate themselves to their new condition.

Autumn Crocus. Pot up now for flowers within a month.

Azaleas. Prune and bring indoors to a cool north window.

Cactus. A cold, light or sunny spot and water but twice a month is preferred while a warm room and weekly watering is tolerated.

Calla, yellow. Don't forget it is still in seclusion outside. Bring indoors and let its rest continue for nearly two months.

Gardenia. Discontinue its manure feedings unless new growth is forming. Syringe tops frequently, especially these first weeks indoors. Water once weekly by pot immersion and in between according to the "feel of the soil."

Geraniums. Select a few of the best budded summer pot plants for autumn window garden effect. Give these a liquid manure tonic later this month. Stir the top soil. Bring into a room where windows are open for many hours during the first two weeks.

Geraniums, scented-leaved. Make cuttings of rose, lemon or any of the other scented types. They will do just as well if not better in water than in soil.

Heliotrope. If this intrigues you, take up some garden plants of it early this month and accustom them to a restricted root system in pots, while there is still nearly a month of humid outdoor growing.

Jasmine (Jasmine grandiflorum). Prune back and trim out dead wood. Since it is now entering its resting period, keep it as cool as possible (40 to 55° F.) and water only sparingly.

Paperwhite Narcissus. Order large bulbs immediately and when they arrive, spread out on a dry sunny window sill for further ripening.

Strelitzia. Bring it inside late this month for a cold, dim rest cure until new leaves begin to appear.

Get your house plants indoors before nights turn cool. They will need a scrubbing and syringing first and maybe an insecticide spraying if you notice any pests. Don't bring in the dying. If they didn't thrive outside, they never will in.

OCTOBER

Amaryllis. Leave outside until after the first *light* frost. Inside, let it go dry until foliage can be cleaned off. Then store the pot in a dark cool place, watering once in three weeks.

Calla Lilies. Why not order a few of the unusuals

like the pink (rehmanni) or the black and yellow (melanoleuca) or a few baby whites which planted immediately should be in flower at poinsettia time.

Christmas Cactus. Be firm. This plant needs a whole month of rest. Set in a dim, cool place and withhold water entirely.

Dutch Bulbs. Pot up any hardy bulbs you intend to force this winter indoors. If you have left-over tulips and daffodils from last winter's indoor display, plant these now in full sun in a fertile garden bed. This will recondition them for outdoor use, anyway.

Easter Lilies. Pot these as soon as they can be procured. Water once and store them in a cold dim place.

Geraniums. Feed young plants twice monthly until the end of April. Retire older plants to a light 50° F. spot as budding ceases by the end of the month. Water once weekly or less. Prune to approximately three pieces of three-inch growth.

Hyacinth, French Roman. Plant in pebbles and water the first of the month and set away in a cool (60° F. or less) spot for eight weeks of rooting.

Hydrangea. Before frost, bring the tender varieties into a cold (40° F.) dim place and water until January about once a month.

Lachenalia and Veltheimia. Pot these unusual and interesting tender bulbs now.

Narcissus. Just before the middle of the month make the first plantings of paperwhites and set in a cool dark place for about three weeks. Keep the water level no higher than the lower third of the bulbs.

Orange and Lemon Trees. These need a cool location and little water from now on for four months.

Marica. Hold the tips frequently under the full stream of an open faucet. This keeps them from turning yellow.

Be mindful of ventilation during these first indoor weeks. As long as possible keep windows open for several hours daily. After fires are started, ventilate regularly but cautiously morning and afternoon.

NOVEMBER

African Violet. Turn your plants to keep them shapely. Watch out for mealy bugs. Ventilate indirectly.

Amaryllis. Order now. Obtain six-inch pots and plant immediately on arrival. Set away to root in a dark cool place (50° F.) Water once in seven to ten days.

Annuals from the garden. Discard ageratum, nicotiana, etc., at any time now when they appear on the wane. They have no future.

Begonias, Wax, everblooming varieties. Secure flowering plants as an all-season standby. Pink Pearl and White Pearl are exceptionally good.

Calla, yellow. Pot now in a six-inch container. Then water and move to the cellar for rooting. Absolute darkness is not necessary.

Christmas Cactus. Water only two or three times the whole month and the last week bring it again to the sunny window garden.

Chrysanthemums. Cut back after flowering and plant outside in a coldframe if you wish to save your gift for garden display. Soak at planting time and again two weeks later. After a hard freeze, pile two inches of oak leaves over the crown and close the glass. Or plant in a protected garden corner and cover with a leaf-filled inverted peach basket after a freeze.

Cyclamen. On the 1st and 15th of the month feed all budding plants.

English Ivy. If it is ailing, hold tops under the splashy stream of a faucet for a few minutes daily. This has a marvelous reconditioning effect. But turn the plant sideways for the operation since ivies prefer a soil which dries out a little between waterings.

Funkia. Dig up a garden clump of funkia and store in a coldframe or cool sunporch for midwinter forcing.

Gardenia. Daily showering of tops is a fine thing.

Geraniums. Prune all summer-weary plants now (not the young *new* ones) back to three inches and place for a three months' rest in a dim cold (45 to 50° F.) spot. Water about once in seven to ten days. (Do not shake off soil and hang by the roots from the cellar ceiling. This is certain death in the modern basement.)

Heliotrope. Watch for white fly. Segregate any affected plants and see what a much colder room and daily Black Leaf 40 sprays will do. (Or just throw the plant out. It has never been a star performer in the house.)

Hyacinths, Dutch singles in glasses. Plant and put away in a dark, cold place but remember to add more water as evaporation takes place. (Allow ten to twelve rooting weeks.)

Narcissus. Bring these after three weeks of cold rooting for two weeks of forcing for Thanksgiving. Plant the Christmas crop about the twentieth. Root these too in cool darkness.

Poinsettia. Start fortnightly schedule of feeding. And continue until bracts show color.

Roses. Purchase miniature roses such as Tom Thumb and Pixie or dig them from the garden and pot in a mixture of garden soil and peatmoss plus a little dried manure. Place in coldframe until cold weather.

Keep all faded blossoms picked and remember that the bi-monthly syringing is a sanitation measure worth a shelf of pest remedies. Remember to drop a piece of charcoal into every container that holds a house plant or bulb growing in water.

DECEMBER

Amaryllis. Don't forget it. Out of sight must not be out of mind. Water is necessary once in seven to ten days.

Christmas Cactus. As new tip growth appears, increase watering to about once a week, then two or three times, never more. As buds form, check. Feed from beginning of growing period every ten days until buds show color. Then stop.

Clivia. Move to a cold (about 50° F.) spot for a rest until February. Water sparingly but don't forget it.

Cyclamen. A cold spot (50 to 60° F.) for new plants and a pebble-filled saucer, please. Give liquid manure feedings every fortnight to new and held over cyclamens from the time the first bud appears until the last flower unfolds.

Hyacinths, French Roman. Bring the bowls of rooted bulbs to sun and warmth (not above 65° F.) the first week in the month. They should bloom for Christmas.

Palms. Don't get so busy this month you forget to keep the jardiniere clean and sweet and the palm fronds regularly sponged free of dust and lurking pests.

Poinsettia. A light, free-from-draught 65° F. location is best, and plenty of water.

Strelitzia. As soon as new leaves appear return to full sun and warmth (to 70° F.) and water and feed.

The florist has a wealth of lovely blooming material this month. Add a few seasonal plants to enhance your own pleasant color scheme — pink poinsettia with your white begonias or a red one with your rosy varieties, a pink cyclamen to place among your purple African violets or a feathery white heather among the constant green of the ferns.

Make your window garden a dominant picture. First polish the glass and wash the shelves and give the plants a good showering before you get too holiday-busy. Then place candles for Christmas Eve burning and a madonna and angels to express the spirit of the season. To you and all who pass, your window will give pleasure. A night picture of it would make a nice personal Christmas card for next year.

✻ ✻

SOURCES OF MATERIAL

The first places to look for shelves, brackets and accessories for constructing a window garden are the local shops. Both hardware and department stores carry a selection, the department stores in particular stocking a larger variety from October through December. The catalogues of some seed firms also list brackets, pots, and certain kinds of containers as well as tools, fertilizers and other necessary equipment.

Local florist shops, greenhouses and nurseries are also the first places to look for house plants. The range in both species and varieties fluctuates with the locality and the year. Again for bulbs and seeds of house plants, we advise you to turn to the catalogue of your favorite seed or bulb dealer. But while the importance of the local greenhouse cannot be overemphasized, you may wish to search farther afield. Here are some suggestions:

Bulbs (spring and fall kinds)

Barnes Importers, The, East Aurora, N. Y.

Flowerfield Bulb Farm, Flowerfield, L. I., N. Y. (fall bulbs; in spring, some house plants)

Garden Center, 53 La Salle Rd., West Hartford 7, Conn. (also seeds)

Houdyshel, Cecil, 1412 Third St., La Verne, Calif.

Schling, Max, Seedsmen, Inc., 618 Madison Ave., N. Y.

Wayside Gardens, Mentor, Ohio

Plants

Adams, I. Sherman, Co., Wellesley, Mass. (orchids)

Charmaine Gardens, 301 Allamanda Dr., Lakeland, Fla. (orchids)

Fruitland Nurseries, Augusta, Ga. (camellias)

Glen St. Mary Nurseries, Glen St. Mary, Fla. (African violets, sweet olive, and others)

Holmes Nursery, Tampa, Fla. (gardenias, jasmines, plumbago, shrimp plant, camellias, and others)

Lager and Hurrell, Summit, N. J. (orchids)

North Street Greenhouses, Danielson, Conn. (begonias, geraniums, and others)

Roehrs, Julius, and Son, East Rutherford, N. J. (bromeliads, foliage plants, also African violets)

Shaffer Nurseries, Clearwater, Fla. (list similar to Holmes Nursery)

Schmidt Nursery, 308 Chestnut Ave., Palo Alto, Calif. (geraniums)

Tinari Floral Gardens, Bethayres, Pa. (African violets)

Village Hill Nursery, Williamsburg, Mass. (geraniums, and other plants)

Seeds

Burgess Seed and Plant Co., Galesburg, Mich.

Friendly Gardens, New Bedford, Penna. (African violet seeds, also leaves)

Henderson, Peter, & Co., Cortlandt St., N. Y., N. Y.

Pearce, Rex, Moorestown, N. J.

Vaughan's Seed Store, 10 West Randolph St., Chicago, Ill.

PLANTS IN THE PHOTOGRAPHS

Frontispiece: On the pebble tray and shelves, Geranium
Olympic Red with Pittsburgh Ivy; Philodendron cordatum
on brackets; Vitis rhombifolia (Grape Ivy) trained on wire
for frame. *Primrose*

Portfolio — 1: Forecast of Spring. On the pebble tray and
shelves, Begonia semperflorens and Primula malacoides;
Philodendron cordatum on brackets; Vitis rhombifolia
(Grape Ivy) trained on wire for frame. *Kangaroo Vine*

    2: A Mantel Study in Enduring Green. Cissus antarctica
at either end; dish garden of succulents and tray of
Peperomias.

    3: Welcome the Guest. Cyclamen in flower; Pittsburgh
Ivy and a bowl of sprouting Narcissus polyanthus.

    4: Thanksgiving. On the radiator cover (heat turned off)
bean pots Zebrina pendulosa, English Ivy and African
Violets, flanked by yellow Chrysanthemums from the
florist. Window sill, African Violets. First shelf, more
Violets, rooted cuttings of Begonia semperflorens
and bowl of Narcissus polyanthus; above Saxifraga
sarmentosa (Strawberry Begonia) with top shelf and
frame of Philodendron cordatum in soil and water.

    5: Christmas. On radiator cover Narcissus polyanthus,
Poinsettia and Pittsburgh Ivy. Window sill and first
shelf, Kalanchoes. Second shelf, Poinsettias, English
Ivy. Top shelf and frame, Kalanchoes and Philodendron cordatum.

    6: Valentine's Day. On radiator cover pots of Zebrina

pendulosa and Cyclamen. First shelf, African Violets and English Ivy. Second shelf, Kalanchoes and vases with Forget-me-nots. Top shelf, Kalanchoes and Philodendron cordatum.

7: Winter Sunshine. Window sill, white Calla Lilies and Daffodils, variety King Alfred. First shelf, Begonia semperflorens, Roman Hyacinths. Second shelf, English Ivy, variegated Peperomia, Philodendron cordatum. Top shelf, Philodendron cordatum, Sansevieria.

8: Orchid at Home. Cypripedium variety.

9: Book Case Ending. Ardisia, Pittosporum and variegated Anthericum.

10: Bright Medley. Bookcase, starting from corner, Bouvardia in flower, Spathiphyllum (foliage), Chrysanthemum, Olea fragrans, Anthericum, Primula obconica, species Begonias, Jasminum grandiflorum (foliage against windowpane). Bracket at window, large leaved Begonia. Window sill, Begonia semperflorens, Cyclamen, variegated Philodendron. Small bracket, Passiflora caerulea in water. Window ledge, Rose geranium in bottles.

11: Gay Fruit for Winter. Otaheite Orange, Boston ferns. Christmas Cherries and Pittsburgh Ivy.

12: Conversation Piece. Vitis rhombifolia (Grape Ivy), pink Poinsettias and crested Boston Fern.

13: Variety in Vines. Window sill, Pittsburgh Ivy, Begonia semperflorens. First shelf (left to right), Selaginella, Oxalis, Pick-a-Back, Oxalis, Philodendron cordatum, Selaginella, Pothos. Second shelf, Vitis rhombifolia, Syngonium, Pothos, Passiflora caerulea — in water, Nephthytis, Vitis rhombifolia, Syngonium, Cissus antarctia.

14: Cacti and Succulents. Window sill, Haworthia cymbiformis, Haworthia glabrata, Crassula argentea, Epiphyllum (Christmas Cactus). First shelf, Nyctocereus serpentinus, Gasteria, Opuntia vestita, Peperomia obtusifolia, Opuntia vulgaris. Top shelf, Coryphantha erecta, Stapelia gigantea, Opuntia microdasys, Hereroa nelii.

15: Behind the Scenes. Hanging basket, Philodendron cordatum. Sink, Begonia semperflorens, Pittsburgh Ivy.

GLOSSARY

Axil. This is a geometric matter. The angle between a branch or leaf and the stem from which it springs is termed the axil. It is this space which a mealy bug often considers its natural abode.

Bract. What we most admire in the poinsettia isn't the flower at all but a modified leaf or bract, brilliantly colored.

Corm. This is a short fleshy underground stem rather like a bulb. The cyclamen grows from a corm.

Crock. A broken piece of flower pot is called a crock. If you fit a few pieces in the bottom of a container for a plant to form a drainage area through which water but not soil will pass, you call it "crocking."

Cut Back. When plants seem to overreach themselves and their growth becomes leggy, long, weak and usually unattractive, as the geranium or wax begonia at the end of the winter, they are relieved of top growth to within an inch or so of the soil. This is called cutting back. It has a healthy, rehabilitating effect.

Cutting. This is a piece cut or broken from a parent plant, usually from younger end growth, and inserted in water, soil or sand until new roots form. In this way additional plants of the identical type of the parent are obtained. Sometimes short lengths of root are used. These are termed root cuttings in contrast to pieces of top growth or stem cuttings.

Dormant. When a plant is inactive because of some unfavorable condition outside itself like cold or lack of sun, it is said to be dormant, but when of itself it reaches the end of a growth cycle and a natural season of inactivity occurs due to internal factors (chemical or physiological) it is said to be resting. A dormant plant may be started into growth by moving it from a cool closet to a warm bright window sill. A plant bent on sleeping will usually continue to sleep regardless of how you water or sun it to wake it up.

Florescence. The time a plant stays in bloom is the period of its florescence.

Forcing. When plants are induced to bloom at other than their natural season, they are said to be forced. So if you dig up a clump of bleeding hearts which normally flower outdoors in April and with early warmth and water induce them to bloom in February, you force them. In the same way the florist brings April-flowering daffodils into bloom for Christmas.

Frond. The entire leafy portion of a fern is termed a frond. It differs from a leaf in that reproductive cells develop on its surface. These appear in regular formation on the underside. Don't mistake them for scale.

Humus. More or less decomposed vegetable or animal (not mineral) matter is called humus. It is important for the fertility and water-holding capacity it has. Every good potting soil contains decayed leaves or old manure or rotted plant tops, or all three — in a word, humus.

Inflorescence. The way a flower blooms varies. Sometimes it develops a cluster of color as in the geranium, sometimes a brilliant single effect as in the lily. Either type of flowering may be termed its inflorescence.

Internodes. The spaces between the tiny swellings or points of growth you feel along the stems of plants are called internodes. (See nodes also.)

Leafmold. When partially or almost wholly decayed leaves are mixed with varying amounts of soil, a material results which is called leafmold. In the forest this naturally accumulates under trees. In the garden we obtain leafmold by collecting alternate layers of leaves and soil in a circle of wire anchored behind a big forsythia bush. Leafmold is a valuable addition to any house plant soil mixture since it contributes not only fertility but a water-holding capacity as well. African violets, begonias, ferns and other fine-rooted plants thrive with a liberal allowance of leafmold in the potting soil.

Node. If you run your finger along the stem of a plant you will feel at regular intervals little swellings or joints. These are called nodes. They are the points of growth for leaves and buds. In taking a geranium cutting, for example, you are urged to select pieces of growth with three or four nodes and to make the cut just at the base of one of them.

Pan. This is a broad, shallow flower pot, good for seed growing indoors but especially used for growing bulbs.

Petiole. The leaf stalk which joins a leaf to a main stem is the petiole. In rooting African violet leaves, for example, it is the petiole which is inserted in sandy soil.

Pinch. If with thumb and finger you nip out the end growth of a branch or remove tight little buds to make development fuller or to delay flowering, you are "pinching" it.

Potbound. When a plant actually fills with roots the container in which it is growing, we say it is potbound and needs more root room. If the pot is lifted from such a plant, a potbound condition is indicated by a mass of roots covering the outside of the soil in a frantic search for food.

Plunge. When you sink the flower pots in which plants are growing up to their rims in the soil of an outdoor bed, you are plunging them. Such is a safer summer practice than removing pots and letting roots range.

Prune. When you cut off part of a plant to keep it shapely or almost all of it to induce fresh new growth from the roots, you are pruning it.

Repotting. See *Shifting.*

Rest Period. See *Dormant.*

Shifting. Installing a plant in a next larger size container with a little more soil but the least possible disturbance is termed shifting. This is in contrast to repotting which may involve replacement of worn-out soil with a fresh mixture, the improvement of drainage conditions and even some cutting back of roots. Shifting is for healthy young plants on their way to maturity. Repotting is for established plants in need of reconditioning. In repotting a larger pot may be provided, the same one used again, or even a smaller one selected, if the pot in which the plant grew was so overlarge that it suffered indigestion from too much soil and water for its size.

Spadix. This is a form of spike in which the actual flowers on a plant are inconspicuously imbedded. On the calla or anthurium the spadix is a very noticeable poker-like spike.

Spathe. In the calla and anthurium the spathe is the showy, colorful part. It is a kind of leaf-like hood growing around and bending over the spadix. It is often mistaken for part of the flower.

Syringing. This is the good practice of lightly cleansing and refreshing the top of a plant by sprinkling it with clear water forced through a bulb syringe or small compression pump.

INDEX